SYNE

VS.

SPHERES OF INFLUENCE
IN THE PAN-EUROPEAN SPACE

Report prepared for the
Policy Planning Staff of the
Federal Foreign Office of Germany

MICHAEL EMERSON
WITH
ARIANNA CHECCHI, NORIKO FUJIWARA,
LUDMILA GAJDOSOVA, GEORGE GAVRILIS
AND ELENA GNEDINA

CENTRE FOR EUROPEAN POLICY STUDIES

BRUSSELS

The Centre for European Policy Studies (CEPS) is an independent policy research institute based in Brussels. Its mission is to produce sound analytical research leading to constructive solutions to the challenges facing Europe today. CEPS Paperbacks present analysis and views by leading experts on important questions in the arena of European public policy, written in a style geared to an informed but generalist readership.

The views expressed in this report are attributable only to the authors, and not to the Federal Foreign Office of Germany, or its Policy Planning Staff.

This report was completed on 7 April 2009.

About the authors

Michael Emerson is Associate Senior Research Fellow at CEPS.

Arianna Checchi is Research Fellow at CEPS.

Noriko Fujiwara is Research Fellow at CEPS.

Ludmila Gajdosova is Executive Director of the Network of Institutes and Schools of Public Administration in Central and Eastern Europe (NISPAcee), Bratislava

George Gavrilis is International Affairs Fellow at the Council for Foreign Relations, New York.

Elena Gnedina is Visiting Research Fellow at CEPS, and PhD candidate at the Queen's University, Belfast.

ISBN 978-92-9079-871-2

Centre for European Policy Studies
Place du Congrès 1, B-1000 Brussels
Tel: 32 (0) 2 229.39.11 Fax: 32 (0) 2 219.41.51
e-mail: info@ceps.eu
internet: http://www.ceps.eu

CONTENTS

EXECUTIVE SUMMARY AND CONCLUSIONS

This report investigates whether and how the EU might, in its policies towards Russia, the Eastern partner countries and Central Asia, build stronger common programmes and projects across these three political 'spaces'. The aim would be to secure synergies between actions that are presently segmented between these three spaces, and especially to induce Russia to become a genuinely cooperative positive-sum-game player in the wider European neighbourhood, rather than to continue its efforts to rebuild the former Soviet Union space as its sphere of influence.

It has to be emphasised at the outset that this is both a major strategic objective and an extremely difficult challenge. Russia's political mind-set and actual policies in recent times have clearly given priority to rebuilding its would-be sphere of influence. The political values and activities of the European Union are seen by Russia as a threat both at home, with risks of contagion from the colour revolutions, and in the East European neighbourhood where the EU appears as a competing and expansionist actor. At the same time Russia is itself quite widely viewed in the EU as a threat as much as a partner, especially in the aftermath of the August 2008 war in Georgia and the two successive interruptions in 2006 and 2009 of gas supplies transiting Ukraine.

Moreover, Russia, Ukraine and other countries of the region have for different political reasons a sharp aversion to anything that would make them feel they were all 'in the same box' in EU foreign policies. The latest development of the European Neighbourhood Policy (ENP), with the proposed regional-multilateral dimension to the Eastern Partnership (EaP), could harden the compartmentalisation of the EU's policies between the Eastern region and Russia. The institutional arrangements now being proposed for the EaP's regional-multilateral activities have provisions for its possible extension to third countries such as Russia and Turkey, but the terms being proposed for this suggest an uncertain and ad hoc association.

Political framework – a Pan-European Dimension

A strategy by the EU to engineer a change in outlook and behaviour on the part of Russia, and also to overcome the suspicions and hostilities towards Russia in a number of East European states, would have to be built upon a substantial set of actions that would deliver clear and concrete benefits, going beyond bureaucratic refinements of EU programmes. Otherwise, a marginal effort employing token instruments would carry no realistic expectation of strategic results.

The political framework for such an initiative could be constructed by adapting and building upon current initiatives and tendencies in EU policies towards the wider European area.

The EU's new Eastern Partnership initiative could prove pivotal in this regard, notably as regards its multilateral-regional aspect. The Commission proposed that third countries such as Russia and Turkey "could be included an ad hoc basis". On 19-20 March 2009, the European Council adopted a somewhat more open formulation. Inclusion of both Russia and Turkey could be generally welcomed, but subject to a degree of 'variable geometry' flexibility depending on the specific actions. The possible inclusion of Russia and Turkey in this multilateral-regional framework will in any case be without prejudice to the specific nature of the bilateral relations that the EU has with each EaP state, or for that matter Russia as strategic partner and Turkey as candidate state. A generally open position could also facilitate the EU's inclusion in the Caucasus Stability Platform recently launched by Turkey, which so far includes Russia but not the EU.

With these adjustments to the Commission's proposal, the way would be open to rationalise the Black Sea Synergy initiative with the regional-multilateral dimension of the Eastern Partnership, thus eliminating a source of potential confusion.

The option of ad hoc third country inclusion in this Eastern Partnership activity could also be reserved for one or more Central Asian states, depending on the topic, noting for example Kazakhstan's 'Path to Europe' initiative. In addition the emerging economic and security links between Europe via Central Asia through to South and East Asia become new horizons for European and Asian policy-makers. This should mean an important evolution in the approach of the EU's Central Asia strategy: the region should be considered not so much as the EU's outer periphery (or 'neighbours of the neighbours' in the words of some EU documents) but rather as a strategic bridge between Europe and China.

To give a firmer political framework to this initiative we use the term 'Pan-European Dimension' to mean cooperative actions between the EU and cross-regional groupings between Russia, Eastern Partners and Central Asian states; involving the EU either with states from each of these three 'spaces', or from at least two of them.[1] There would be 'variable geometry' in the participation of specific actions. Actions involving the EU and states for just one other of the 'spaces' would be handled under the bilateral relations between the EU and the states concerned, or the EaP, or Central Asia strategy. These arrangements would be preferable to the hypothesis of extending the activity to the entire CIS space, which would encounter various political objections.

The EU has become highly creative in devising 'regional dimensions' in its relations with different parts of its wider neighbourhood. The Northern Dimension is the case that uses this term, yet the Union for the Mediterranean, Eastern Partnership, Black Sea Synergy, Central Asia strategy and recent Arctic initiative are all variants on this theme.

What has so far been missing is a Pan-European Dimension, targeting actions that optimally overarch several regions or spaces. It would not be necessary or desirable to create a new institutional structure for the Pan-European Dimension. However it would be open for any state, or group of states to advance proposals for consideration, and to be explored in bilateral meetings with the EU, as well in the framework of the regional-multilateral component of the Eastern Partnership.

The functional utility of a Pan-European Dimension has of course to be demonstrated. With this in mind the larger part of the present report reviews a set of possible 'flagship projects' in the economic, energy, climate change, civil society and security domains. The political case for the EU to explore the potential of such an initiative at the present time is clear enough. There is an urgent need for confidence-building measures especially between the EU, Russia and the Eastern Partner states in the aftermath of the war in Georgia, the Ukraine gas crisis and the global economic crisis. There is a need to develop the Eastern Partnership, but also to avoid its becoming a source of greater compartmentalisation of Europe. There is a need to respond constructively to President Medvedev's call for a pan-European security architecture, which so far is conspicuously lacking

---

[1] Possible combinations include: EU-Russia-EaP-CA, EU-Russia-EaP, EU-EaP-CA or EU-Russia-CA.

in concrete substance coming from either Russia or the EU. There is a need for a political framework to bring together a substantial set of 'flagship actions' as a coherent strategic initiative in order to secure economic and political synergetic benefits.

On how such a Pan-European Dimension might be initiated, there is no reason to depart from the EU's regular procedure: the European Council might invite the Commission to draw up a Communication on the subject within a reasonable delay such as six months. However the proposed adjustment of the formula for participation in the regional-multilateral part of the Eastern Partnership would best be prepared in time for the forthcoming official launch of the EaP at a summit meeting in May 2009.

Flagship projects

With this in mind, the present report examines various sectors of policy for the opportunities that they might present for cooperative action between the EU, Russia, Eastern Europe and Central Asia. The list is selective, but also fairly exhaustive in that it is hard to think of other policy sectors that could offer more promising potential for the purpose at hand.

1. **Trade.** The idea of a Pan-European Economic Space is a first candidate for consideration because it can be based on strong existing EU competences; moreover there is currently momentum in favour of extending the EU's network of free trade agreements in the European neighbourhood. Negotiations for Deep Free Trade Agreements (DFTA) are underway or envisaged with the Eastern partners, and the idea of a Common European Economic Space has often featured in political discourse. In addition, the Commission has expressed its interest in a FTA with Russia. But here there is a blockage, first with Russia's failure yet to join the WTO, with opposition within Russia to an FTA with the EU, which some consider would mainly be to the EU's advantage. The current global recession is intensifying Russian protectionist tendencies (e.g. already for cars). The counter-argument is that Russia's economic policy is failing to develop a diversified and competitive industrial economy, and that at some point trade liberalisation with the EU will need to be part of the remedial therapy.

2. **Transport.** The pan-European transport infrastructure and networks have been the subjects of intensive planning for almost two decades, with the successful (consensual) identification of priority axes or corridors. Relatively large sums are being invested by the EU institutions and national governments in the intra-EU networks. Their

extension beyond the EU into Eastern Europe and Central Asia progresses much less quickly, due to lesser funding and various bureaucratic and political obstacles. A new development is seen in plans for Eurasian land connections with corridors stretching East from Central Asia supported by the Asian Development Bank, which could be linked to EU supported projects. The recently decided extension of the European Investment Bank's mandate to operations in Central Asia will be helpful in this context.

3. **Energy.** For the purpose of the present study, seeking synergies from cooperative projects between the EU, Russia, Eastern Europe and Central Asia, the gas pipeline network options are of inescapable importance. There are now five major pipelines, actual or planned, that come into play: the two main land routes from Russia transiting through Ukraine and Belarus, the Nord and South Stream projects that would avoid transit countries before reaching the EU, and the Nabucco/Southern Corridor being promoted by the EU. Of these a reconfiguration of the Ukrainian trunk pipeline, with a long-term concession leased to a tripartite (EU-RUS-UKR) consortium, could offer outstanding economic and political benefits. The Nabucco/Southern Corridor plans also open up tripartite (EU, Eastern Europe, Central Asia) cooperative possibilities, which could conceivably become quadripartite if Russia accepted the offer to join.

4. **Water-hydro-energy-food crisis in Central Asia.** Since the collapse of the Soviet Union, cooperative management of the water, hydro-electric and irrigation resources of Central Asia has catastrophically broken down, resulting in growing humanitarian distress in upstream Kyrgyzstan and Tajikistan through lack of winter heating, and in downstream Uzbekistan and Turkmenistan through water shortages for agriculture. The resulting internal and intra-state tensions are growing, and could lead to open conflicts. The alert is being sounded by international agencies, but to little effect. The EU cannot itself become the main architect of a solution, but it could help shape a coalition of all major actors to this end, and use its weight in the board of the World Bank to advocate a more pro-active approach.

5. **Climate change**. Three countries – Russia, Ukraine and Kazakhstan – are especially heavy polluters, particularly through their use of coal and obsolete energy-using technologies. They will resist inclusion in the group of advanced countries making ambitious and binding quantitative commitments at the climate change talks in Copenhagen at

the end of 2009. However the EU could propose a collaborative action with these three countries together setting up a Quadripartite Climate Change Dialogue, Concretely this could assist the development of national Emissions Trading Schemes, and the amplification of conventional energy efficiency and saving programmes, leading on to collaborative projects for carbon capture and storage (CCS) pilot projects.

6. **Border management**. The EU and its member states are already active in the field of border management in Eastern Europe and Central Asia. The challenges in Central Asia, with the drug trails from Afghanistan, are especially daunting. The main EU efforts are in the Border Management Programme for Central Asia (BOMCA) mission, which however is operated by UNDP, with a lack of EU visibility. Detailed proposals are made below for the EU to establish regional border assistance centres in Central Asia and the Caucasus, with funds to amplify operations, and openings for Russia and third parties to join in.

7. **Conflict resolution and civil emergencies.** The conflict resolution and prevention agenda in East European states is an obvious candidate in theory for EU-Russian collaboration, together with the interested third states directly concerned (in the South Caucasus, Transnistria and Crimea). Russia has taken the view, however, that the perpetuation of these conflicts was in its tactical geo-political interest, until and unless circumstances such as the August war with Georgia presented the opportunity for decisive 'victory'. However this policy has contributed heavily to Russia's poor reputation in European affairs. In the hypothesis of this paper, Russia might be induced to change this stance, and join with the EU in genuine conflict resolution and prevention efforts, in which case there could be a remarkable turnaround in favour of cooperative outcomes. A Pan-European Civil Emergencies Facility is also proposed.

8. **Civil society and political development.** A set of three networks in the broad civil society and public policy field illustrates how it is possible to organise politically sensitive activity overarching the former Soviet bloc, from Eastern Europe to Central Asia. These networks are plausible candidates for stronger support by the EU, member states and European private international foundations. The sums suggested, totalling €25 million for all three networks, would mean a substantial increase in present funding, but these are not large sums in relation to total resources available under the European Neighbourhood and

Partnership Instrument (ENPI), the funding instrument of the EU's European Neighbourhood Policy.

9. **Pan-European security.** President Medvedev has proposed a new pan-European security architecture, which sounds promising at first sight. However the credibility of Russia's intentions has been undermined by its behaviour in the war with Georgia and its recognition of Abkhazia and South Ossetia. While the Medvedev speeches have not so far referred to the Organisation for Security and Cooperation in Europe (OSCE), whose 'Helsinki principles' must serve as the normative foundations of any such architecture, it is positive that discussions are now taking place within OSCE fora. The EU and NATO are reflecting on how to respond. The EU might respond by taking steps itself to reinforce the OSCE: first, for the EU (post-Lisbon) to become a full member of the OSCE; and second, in order to limit the heavy constraints of meetings of all 56 member states, for it to test the ground for possible core group meetings (e.g. tripartite EU-Rus-US). As and when confidence has been improved between the parties, to propose consideration of a new European Security Council which would be a core group of major players within the OSCE (this could be a variant on a long-standing request from Moscow).

10. **Other pan-European multilateralism.** The several pan-European multilateral organisations should in principle be supporting cooperation between all parties. Of the existing organisations only the European Bank for Reconstruction and Development (EBRD) has established an important niche activity that all parties, including Russia, seem content to work with. On the other hand, Russia seeks to marginalise or ignore other organisations that should be serving key functions (especially the Energy Charter Treaty and the OSCE), while the United Nations Economic Commission for Europe (UNECE) and Black Sea Economic Cooperation (BSEC) find it difficult to sustain or build significant roles. Both the OSCE and BSEC could see their role in economic affairs enhanced by several of the proposals discussed here. The recent gas crisis poses the question whether should be fresh negotiations over revision or enhancement of the Energy Charter Treaty.

11. **The global financial and economic crisis.** The financial and economic crisis is deepening in Eastern Europe and Central Asia, which sees Russia rushing in with financial aid to several countries of the region, alongside interventions by the IMF, with the EU deciding also to

augment the financial instruments that it can deploy. All this makes a case for coordinated responses in cases such as Ukraine, including conditionalities, in order to avoid inconsistent actions and to secure synergetic benefits. Such coordination between Russia on the one hand, and the IMF, EU and the countries concerned on the other, is not yet happening. Perhaps initiatives along these lines could be engineered.

Conclusions

The current global financial and economic crisis might lead to a rethink in Russia over its strategic attitudes, to which President Obama's newly declared wish for a fresh start with Russia may also contribute. No longer under the delusion of 'holding all the cards', Russia may become more open to propositions of cooperation of the type discussed in this paper. But that certainly cannot be taken for granted. While the hypothetical actions reviewed in this report objectively offer possibilities for improving the status quo, almost all of them would currently encounter political obstacles for their realisation. The tantalising idea is that the current crisis might become the tipping point to set in motion a change of strategic attitudes and thence a cascade of cooperative actions of the kinds outlined in this report.

The incentives offered to Russia lie first in the intrinsic value of a series of concrete economic and security projects. The overall Pan-European Dimension would provide a political framework of bilateral and regional-multilateral relations in line with Russia's aspirations to play a leading role in the wider Europe. Developments along these lines would also reinvigorate the bilateral EU-Russia relationship, and provide a favourable context in which to conclude an ambitious new agreement to succeed the Partnership Cooperation Agreement (PCA).

Summary of flagship projects for cross-regional cooperation in the Pan-European Space

- Pan-European free trade area
- Coordination of EU-Rus-IFIs macro-financial assistance in Eastern Europe
- Extension of European Investment Bank mandate to Central Asia (initiated)
- Pan-European transport corridors to link from Central to East & South Asia
- Tripartite Ukr-EU-Rus corporate restructuring of Ukraine transit pipeline
- Cooperative rationalisation of Nabucco/Southern Corridor/South Stream
- CA-Rus-EU-IFIs cooperation over Central Asian water/hydro power nexus
- Quadripartite EU-Rus-Ukr-Kazak climate change dialogue
- Quadripartite EU-Rus-Ukr-Kazak carbon capture and storage pilot projects,
- EU border management projects in Central Asia and the Caucasus, with Russia
- EU-Rus Civil Emergencies Cooperation Framework for Pan-European Space
- EU and private foundations to strengthen pan-European civil society networks
- Reform of OSCE as key to pan-European security architecture

PART I
PRINCIPLES AND PARADIGMS

1. INTRODUCTION

The subject of this study is the pursuit of coherence and possible synergies in EU policies towards Russia, the Eastern neighbourhood states and Central Asia. These three 'dimensions' are currently subject to EU policies that have quite a lot in common, but are nonetheless in separate policy-making categories.

The question is whether the effectiveness of these policies could be enhanced by bringing them closer together in various operational ways. These sets of EU neighbourhood policies are differentiated for clear political reasons, yet there is a strong thread of commonality among them based on the EU's operational tools and political values.

The strategic issue is over what paradigm of international relations may or should prevail across this vast region, as between two models:

- A space increasingly and clearly divided between EU and Russian spheres of influence, with more competition and tensions than cooperation over the common East European neighbourhood and Central Asia.

- A space where all parties come to see the advantages of wide-ranging cooperation at least in economic and security spheres, if not also in the political sphere. The parties would effectively obtain synergetic benefits from multiple cooperative endeavours.

The position of the EU is to work towards this second model, whereas the Russian leadership is more heavily oriented towards the first. Is it possible to develop the EU policy agenda in such a way as to induce Russia to see greater advantage in this second desired model?

The background on the EU side is seen in several policy developments, including: the opening of negotiations with Russia over a successor to the Partnership and Cooperation Agreement (PCA), efforts to strengthen the European Neighbourhood Policy (ENP) with the Eastern Partnership (EaP), and the Central Asia strategy. In addition there are several more limited regional initiatives: the Black Sea Synergy, the Northern Dimension and the new Commission paper on the Arctic region.

The political context has of course been greatly sharpened by the combination of the August 2008 war between Georgia and Russia, the renewed breakdown in gas transit through Ukraine in January 2009 and the effects of the global financial and economic crisis.

In our pursuit of coherence and possible synergies in EU policies towards Russia, we have assembled concrete information on sectors of policy, projects and institutional arrangements that may offer potential for multi-regional cooperation in the various possible combinations: all four (EU-Rus-EaP-CA) together, as well as the three-way combinations (EU-Rus-EaP), (EU-Rus-CA) and (EU-EaP-CA).

2. The Clash of Paradigms

While the bulk of this paper addresses mechanisms of EU policy at a concrete and relatively technical level, the link to the overarching strategic purpose has to be kept in perspective. The overarching issue is 'the Russia question', and in particular how to induce Russia to come closer to Europe's worldview and normative conception of the wider European area,[2] and to build a better such convergence with concrete processes and projects of cooperation.

The contemporary European (EU) view of itself corresponds to what the international relations literature calls 'European international society', which has been defined as:

> when a group of states, conscious of certain common interests and common values, form a society in the sense that they conceive themselves to be bound by a common set of rules in their relations with each other, and share in the working of common institutions.[3]

This is a fair description of the EU-centred Europe, but not one in which today's Russia could be recognised. Russia has for centuries been struggling to define itself in relation to Europe. While there have been some phases, from Peter the Great to the early post-Soviet period, when Russia attempted to converge on European norms, these have proved to be thin and short-lived. The dominant historical picture is one of Russia perceiving itself as a great power that sets its own norms and controls its own imperial space. These characteristics were seen during various Tsarist regimes and then in their most extreme form, especially in terms of an own normative

---

[2] An excellent survey of the ideational bases and contradictions in the Russia-EU relationship is by Hiski Haukala, "Multi-causal Social Mechanisms and the Study of International Institutionalisation: The Case of the EU-Russia Strategic Partnership", University of Turku, doctoral dissertation, 2008, Turku.

[3] Hedley Bull, *The Anarchical Society: A Study of Order in World Politics*, Oxford: Oxford University Press, 1977, 1995.

ideology and control of empire, in the Communist period. While the Communism has gone, today's leadership group is still coming substantially from the ranks of the Soviet KGB, and exhibits these same enduring traits in their approach to European and international affairs.

Russia is special of course by virtue of its size (the biggest nation in Europe) and economic structure (its huge natural resource base), but the most relevant characteristic for the present study is its view of itself in Europe and the world, which tends to be the categorical opposite of the modern (or post-modern) Europe of the European Union. Russia's leadership defines the state as a great power, boasts its military strength as a nuclear power (flying strategic bombers to Venezuela last summer) and relishing the chance to use its conventional military hardware (as in the August war with Georgia). Its military is in fact in large measure greatly weakened by the low level of technical quality of its weaponry and by dreadful standards of morale and behaviour in the lower ranks (conditions for conscripts), but it champions its military strength in annual displays in Red Square, and in continuing celebration of the Great Patriotic War. These expressions of nationalist patriotism are a key part of the authoritarian leadership's propaganda efforts to justify its own legitimacy, and to cover up the grave weaknesses of the economy and social system, and also the huge corruption of the ruling class with their increasing control of major enterprises.

Continuing the national discourse, it is further alleged that the West exploited Russia's moment of weakness and humiliated it after the collapse of the Soviet Union, for example with NATO's expansion into the former Soviet space. Russia engages in an extremely convoluted foreign policy discourse, claiming the moral high ground in referring to the 'illegal' actions of the US (or West) in Kosovo and Iraq, while then quoting the Kosovo example as justification for its own recognition of the independence of Abkhazia and South Ossetia.[4] It blocks or weakens the actions of the OSCE and Council of Europe in the domain of democracy, while claiming to have its own model of ('sovereign') democracy. It claims to be searching for peaceful solutions to the unresolved conflicts of the former Soviet space, but operates tactically in all the cases in point

---

[4] For a frank Russian view, see Andrei Makarychev, *Russia and its 'New Security Architecture' in Europe: A Critical Examination of the Concept*, CEPS Policy Brief, January 2009.

(Transnistria, Abkhazia, South-Ossetia, and Nagorno Karabakh) in pursuit of manifest *realpolitik* objectives. It sees opportunities to stir up trouble in Crimea; for example Moscow's 'vertical of power' does nothing to restrain Mayor Lushkov from inflaming tensions over the Black Sea fleet and Sevastopol.

Russia's economy has been undergoing bewilderingly huge swings in its fortunes, from the initial post-Soviet collapse, to recovery in the mid-1990s, but then the 1998 financial crash, on to a decade of rapid growth and enrichment which culminated in mid-2008 with Russia perceiving itself as holding all the cards, while China and the West scrambled for scarce mineral resources, followed now in the great 2008-09 global financial and economic crisis that is now humbling Russia once again. The strategic consequences of the current global crash cannot yet be seen clearly. Yet we know that this is the gravest economic crisis since the Great Depression of the 1930s, which itself resulted in the advance of the welfare state, the rise of fascism, world war, and the post-war order built around the United Nations, the Bretton Woods institutions and the birth and growth of today's European Union. The legacy of that first Great Depression took half a century to be fully revealed. Is the devastating impact of the current global crash going perhaps to shake Russia out of its very old-fashioned (19th century) mode of foreign and security policy? At least the context is changed drastically, and it may open up opportunities to get Russian foreign and security policies onto a fresh track. But there cannot be a presumption that this new weakness in Russia will lead Russian policy in the direction that Europe would like to see: the old model of economic distress inducing leaders to become more populist, nationalist, paranoiac, xenophobic, adventurist-militarist and repressive is still there, available for use.

Conclusion: Russia's urge to restore its position of power in the former Soviet space is deeply entrenched in the mindset and intentions of its leadership; and certainly much more so than ideas of complex cooperative endeavours with the European Union, which it sees as an ambiguous combination of cooperation partner and a competitive expansionist threat. The current global economic crisis is certainly hitting Russia hard, challenging its recent self-perception of fast-growing economic strength, but leaving quite unknown at this stage the possible political scenarios, from adoption of a more cooperative stance in international relations to an even more populist nationalism, deepening the clash of paradigms. Correspondingly, a strategy to induce Russia to switch its outlook and foreign policy behaviour closer to what the EU would consider cooperative and congenial is going to need a very substantial set of projects that deliver clear and concrete benefits, going way beyond various bureaucratic refinements of EU programmes. This will have to be a matter of obtaining strategic leverage with big instruments (for scale, the Schmidt-Brezhnev gas pipeline project offers an apt example); otherwise, it will be nothing more than a marginal effort employing token instruments and carrying no realistic expectation of achieving strategic results.

3. EU POLICIES TOWARDS RUSSIA, EASTERN EUROPE, CENTRAL ASIA AND REGIONAL DIMENSIONS

The EU is currently renewing or strengthening its relations with three areas – Russia, the Eastern neighbours and Central Asia. All three relationships are in a comparatively fluid state at this time, since they are at various stages of policy-shaping and negotiation, each with some degree of freedom for defining the way ahead. The proposed renewal of the EU-Russia Partnership and Cooperation Agreement finally saw the opening of the negotiation process at the end of 2008, after serious hesitations and divisions on the EU side whether or on what conditions to go ahead, given Russia's problematic behaviour in the August war with Georgia, following several earlier incidents (Estonian monument, Polish meat affair, etc.). There have been continuing attempts to strengthen the European Neighbourhood Policy without making new commitments to membership perspectives, from the efforts of the German Presidency in the first half of 2007 through to the current efforts to develop the Eastern Partnership (EaP). The Commission Communication of December 2008 on the EaP opens up a number of ideas to be weighed in the present context, to which we return below. Finally the EU's new 'Central Asia Strategy' was launched in the course of 2007-08.

These three blocks of policy are distinct and separate for quite clear reasons. The ENP/EaP states have a core group (Ukraine, Moldova and Georgia) that aspire to membership perspectives and so are willing to work under the paradigm of convergence on EU norms and standards, and with procedures that resemble the accession process (even while the EU persistently denies membership perspective requests). Thus the ENP Action Plans and Progress Reports are broadly structured according to the chapters of the accession process and the Regular Reports on each candidate. In addition for Ukraine it has been agreed that the next treaty-level agreement will be an 'Association Agreement'. Armenia's leadership makes speeches with European identity content. Azerbaijan is willing to play along with the process, so as not to exclude itself. Belarus increasingly appears also interested in joining in, so to have options in relation to Russia; and this tendency may now be accentuated following the IMF loan to help its economy resist the current crisis.

Russia on the other hand rejects as a matter of political principle the idea of convergence on European norms and standards, although in practice this position has ambiguities and contradictions to it. At the technical level Russian sectoral ministries and various private sector interest groups are often quite open to adopting or drawing on European standards where there is a 'modernisation' advantage to be obtained. And at the political level Russian discourse on controversial foreign and security policy issues (Georgia, Kosovo) is heard invoking the same normative principles as the EU uses to justify its positions (its actions in Georgia have been justified by the precedent set by the EU in Kosovo). Since Russia's principled declarations are subject to such inconsistencies, a more basic explanation may be more relevant, namely that Russia as a major power does not want to be treated by the EU in the same category as 'lesser' former Soviet republics, and rejects in particular the idea of political conditionalities which some of the ENP/EaP states are willing to contemplate. It is evident that both Russia on the one hand, and Ukraine and Georgia on the other, each have their own political reasons for wishing *not* to be grouped together in EU policies.

Finally, the Central Asian states have become increasingly separated from the European neighbours in their relations with the EU, in spite of the fact that in the early post-Soviet period the EU offered them Partnership and Cooperation Agreements on the basis of the model that emerged for the European partner states. This happened for a whole set of basic reasons: geographical and cultural distance, disinterest in democracy in the region, weaker economic integration with the EU, etc. Only recently has the EU begun to try a fresh start with its Central Asia Strategy, and only with Kazakhstan does there now appear a serious interest in closer relations.

Eastern Partnership

The Commission's EaP proposals open up some important new perspectives, with implications for both Russia and Central Asia.[5] These proposals are being discussed with member states at the time of writing. Preliminary orientations were set at the European Council meeting of 19-20 March 2009, and more precise decisions will have to be adopted in time for the EaP's launch summit event in early May 2009.

One of the major proposals for the EaP is the idea of regional-multilateral activity in four domains (democracy, economics, energy and people contacts) for six countries (i.e. Ukr, Mol, Geo, Arm, Azer + Belarus to a certain degree), without however Russia or Central Asia. On the other hand the Commission proposed that 3rd countries "could be involved … on a case by case basis, and if there is agreement" that this would be beneficial. These 3rd countries could include Russia, Turkey and in some instances maybe Kazakhstan. How this 3rd country participation will play out will be of considerable importance in relations to the objectives of the present study, and different scenarios may be imagined. The European Council for its part on 19-20 March 2009 broadly endorsed the Commission's proposals, but with a slightly more open formulation: "Third countries will be eligible for participation on a case by case basis in concrete projects, activities and meetings of thematic platforms, where it contributes to the objectives of particular activities and the general objectives of the Eastern Partnership".[6]

The first question is then whether or how far Russia will be invited to join in all or any of the four thematic groups for regional-multilateral work of the EaP. The invitation process is itself not entirely clear. Differing positions may be presumed, with some new member states and Georgia and Ukraine likely to be the most reserved over Russian participation. The debate will be about the logic of engagement versus the risks that Russia would only be a spoiler. One could expect reservations over Russia's

---

[5] "Eastern Partnership: Communication from the European Commission", COM(2008) 823, 3 December 2008.

[6] Declaration by the European Council on the Eastern Partnership – Annex to EU Presidency Conclusions, 19-20 March.

participation on matters of democracy, but a more positive view on economics, energy and people contacts.

The second question is then whether Russia would want to cooperate, if invited. Russia would surely prefer to participate as an equal party, not as an observer with lesser status. Russia could cite the example of the Northern Dimension initiative, and in particular its 'New Northern Dimension' format since 2007, when it was reshaped into a partnership between the EU, Russia, Norway and Iceland, with operating principles and procedures that stress the equal partnership between all the parties.[7] These questions of how Russia can fit in with wider regional initiatives were also tested at the first Black Sea Synergy ministerial meeting in Kiev early in 2008, with quite instructive results. In the Black Sea context, the question became whether the regional-multilateral activity should be placed either 1) in the institutional setting of the Black Sea Economic Cooperation (BSEC) organisation, or 2) be simply open to BSEC member states together with the EU. Russia and Turkey pushed for the first option, probably for different reasons: Russia, so that it could control developments through the BSEC institutional consensus rule, and Turkey out of *amour propre* for this Istanbul-based organisation. The EU favoured the second option, while being ready also for the Commission to become observer in BSEC. The outcome was actually a compromise, with the ministerial meeting divided into two separate sessions, corresponding to each of the two options. The risk of Russia acting as spoiler is far from being an academic hypothesis, since it has been clearly in evidence in recent times in its policy towards both the OSCE and Council of Europe. Moreover the comparative failure of BSEC to become an effective regional organisation has been ascribed in part to Russia's blocking position on many proposals for action.

The issue posed by these Black Sea affairs is one of technical complexity and political sensitivity for all parties, to the point that the Commission felt it necessary in January 2009 to distribute to member states a 'non-paper' on how to define the respective roles of the Black Sea Synergy

---

[7] P. Aalto, H. Blakkisrud and H. Smith (eds), *The New Northern Dimension of the European Neighbourhood*, CEPS, 2008.

and the regional-multilateral part of the EaP.[8] This latter would be the first instance in which the EU has taken the leadership in an initiative to bring together all the European former Soviet states without Russia – either at all, or only on an ad hoc and discretionary invitation basis. Critics of this initiative could say that it is going in the wrong direction, compared to endeavours in which the EU would try to bring the European CIS states together in a new spirit of cooperation. But to this criticism there is a more subtle counter-argument, which might foresee a sequential game process with Russia. According to this argument Russia is a realistic and pragmatic foreign policy actor, and its behaviour will depend on the context. If Russia sees the opportunity to re-establish a hegemonic or dominant leadership role among the former Soviet states, it will readily exploit this. If on the other hand Russia observes that this is no longer possible, in part because its recent policies have antagonised most of the European former Soviet states, and that the EU is making headway in developing its own political and economic relationship with these states, then it may judge it better to join the process rather than exclude itself. The new EaP initiative, especially in its regional-multilateral aspect, may be seen in this light as a message to Russia that its recent policies has resulted in increasing unity among EU and EaP partner states, and one that creates a new framework that can function without Russia. If this initiative becomes sufficiently substantial and credible then it might be instrumental in changing Russian views of how to pursue its own interests.

As regards links between Eastern Europe and Central Asia there is a special point to be made concerning Kazakhstan, which is the most important state of the region to Europe on several grounds: size, energy resources, proximity and regional leadership potential (as illustrated by its forthcoming OSCE chairmanship). In addition Kazakhstan has made overtures towards the Council of Europe for some kind of a more active relationship. Most notably in 2008, Kazakhstan published a strategy document entitled "The Path to Europe", which quite carefully and pragmatically selected themes for cooperation with the EU. The EU has every interest to support this development. One way to do this would be to

---

[8] "Delineation and Complementarity between the Eastern Partnership and the Black Sea Synergy", 'non-paper' of the European Commission services, 28 January 2009.

encourage Kazakhstan to join the EaP regional-multilateral groups discussed above. More ambitiously Kazakhstan might be invited as an associate of the ENP/EaP process, which could be justified by the argument that Kazakhstan is geographically partly in Europe (like Russia and Turkey). Another way would be to make Kazakhstan the front-runner among Central Asia states for the negotiation of a new agreement to replace the obsolete Partnership and Association Agreement.

While the EU's Central Asia Strategy has got off to a cautious start there are interesting new horizons in prospect with the keen interest of China and the Asian Development Bank in this region, as manifest in the Bank's Central Asia Regional Economic Cooperation (CAREC) programme, which inter alia supports major transport corridors that would go West from East and South Asia towards Europe via Central Asia. There should be a mutual interest on the part of the EU, which sponsors the pan-European corridors that go from the EU to its Eastern periphery, to join up these corridors. More strategically this could see the EU come to view Central Asia not so much as its outer periphery, but more as its bridge into Asia proper.

'Stability Pact' or 'Platform' for the Caucasus

For the South Caucasus there is a return to the question of whether the war in Georgia could have a positive sequel in the shape of a comprehensive initiative for future regional cooperation, perhaps a *Stability Pact for the Caucasus*. This idea surfaced first as a Turkish initiative in 2000, in the wake of the Stability Pact for South East Europe. That initiative was never really worked out at the official level, although this was done unofficially by CEPS.[9]

Turkey returns now with the idea of a *Caucasus Stability and Cooperation Platform,* and hosted a first meeting in Istanbul in January 2009 with five parties present at deputy minister level: Armenia, Azerbaijan, Georgia, Russia and Turkey, but without Abkhazia and South Ossetia (presumably because Georgia would not have accepted to participate otherwise). This restricted participation reflects the growing substance of the Russian-Turkish bilateral relationship, which in the South Caucasus has

---

[9] CEPS published a detailed but unofficial *Stability Pact for the Caucasus*, CEPS, 2000, which was discussed with the leaderships of the South Caucasus and civil society NGOs.

been competitive or conflictual for centuries, but now becomes more collaborative. In particular Russia and Turkey share to a degree the same urge to look after this region themselves as principal actors, while Iran is not invited, and the EU and US are viewed as secondary parties external to the region.

There is little heard so far regarding the substantive activity of the *Platform*. One could imagine that both Russia and Turkey would be interested in investing in good road and rail connections along the Black Sea coast, which would require the cooperation of both Abkhazia (presumably in favour) and Georgia (presumably against). Similarly there are important transport routes through Armenia to Azerbaijan, which are currently blocked by the unresolved Nagorno Karabakh conflict. Both Russia and Turkey have been volunteering their services as mediators over the Nagorno Karabakh question in recent months. Given that Russia has been perceived as Armenia's protector, and Turkey Azerbaijan's, the Russo-Turkish combination could have a serious logic.

If the EU were to sponsor a Stability Pact (or Platform) for the Caucasus it might draw on the experience of the Stability Pact for South East Europe, with three working tables for economics, security and politics, with more specialised sub-groups having proved necessary for practical purposes. A version of this for the Caucasus might be as illustrated in the box below.

Workings of a South Caucasus Stability Pact

Political and institutional

- Establishment of a South Caucasus Community, with a governing Council of the 3 South Caucasus states

    + Associate status for Abkhazia, South Ossetia and Nagorno Karabakh (?)

    + External sponsors, Russia & Turkey; +EU & US (?), Iran (?), OSCE (?)

- A Parliamentary Assembly

Economic policy

- External and intra-regional trade and market integration policies
- Transport infrastructures and coordination
- Energy infrastructure and market coordination

Security

- Security arrangements in and around the former conflict zones

- Security sector reform
- Cooperation over combating organised crime and drug trafficking

People

- Refugee and IDP return and assistance
- Education and youth initiatives
- Inter-ethnic truth and reconciliation initiatives

The Balkan Stability Pact was for almost a decade driven by the EU and the West, but in 2008 was transformed into a regionally-owned organisation, the Regional Cooperation Council. A South Caucasus initiative might follow a similar trajectory, initially relying heavily on external sponsors, later becoming a more autonomous community. On matters of structure, one may suppose that there would be a core Council of the three fully recognised states of the region. The difficulties already encountered in the Geneva talks over how to include Abkhazia and South Ossetia would have to be resolved. There would be also the question of Nagorno Karabakh's possible representation, which would be most easily resolved if it became an autonomous region with a special international status. The Northern Cyprus model may be borne in mind in two respects, benefiting from a degree of functional cooperation (from the EU) without formal recognition, and as a case where the prospect of re-unification may improve after decades of conflictual separation.[10]

While this idea of a Stability Pact or Platform for the Caucasus is of interest, there would have to be choices made in relation to overlapping initiatives, which include the EaP and Black Sea Synergy, and the BSEC organisation. The three states of the region do not seem keen to focus on their 'Caucasus identity', and Georgia and Armenia prefer to build on a wider Black Sea and European identity. This might leave a Caucasus initiative to deal with a modest agenda of technical issues of local cooperation.

Conclusion: The latest development of the European Neighbourhood Policy, with its Eastern Partnership dimension, and its proposed regional-multilateral activity could actually harden the compartmentalisation between the EU's policies towards the Eastern region and Russia. The institutional arrangements now being

---

[10] Cyprus became divided with the Turkish invasion of 1974, and currently after 34 years re-unification prospects have become more promising than ever before.

proposed for the EaP's regional-multilateral activity have provisions for its possible extension to third countries such as Russia and Turkey, but so far the terms for this extension proposed are for an uncertain and ad hoc association. For their part Russia and Turkey are initiating a South Caucasus Platform that would exclude the EU (and US). These developments are contrary to the hypothesis underlying the present report.

On the other hand there is a still the option for the EU to choose a more inclusive formula for the Eastern Partnership, leaving its bilateral activity confined to ENP states, but opening the regional multilateral activity to both Russia and Turkey more clearly. This could allow also rationalisation of the Black Sea Synergy initiative with the regional-multilateral dimension of the Eastern Partnership, which might be reciprocated by an opening of the South Caucasus Platform to the EU.

PART II
SELECTED POLICY DOMAINS
AND INSTITUTIONAL STRUCTURES

4. TRADE POLICY

Trade policy is an inevitable test case for the proposition that there might be a better overarching system of cooperation between the EU, Eastern Europe and Russia, with conceivable extension to Central Asia as well. This follows from several positive pre-conditions: trade is invariably at the heart of any regional integrative initiative, the EU's own position in trade policy is one of leadership, Russia has been trying itself to create a Eurasian economic space but without much success, and finally regional free trade agreements on integration seems to be advancing worldwide alongside the failure of the WTO to reach agreement over the Doha round at the global level.

The EU is currently developing its trade policies towards EaP states in important ways, starting with the current negotiations with Ukraine for a Deep and Comprehensive Free Trade Agreement (DCFTA). Beyond a conventional free trade agreement (FTA), which would just scrap tariffs, the DCFTA will liberalise also service sectors and extend to neighbouring countries a considerable degree of regulatory harmonisation based on that of the EU's internal market. The Commission proposes to follow on from the Ukraine case and use it as a template for further DCFTAs with other EaP states. When there is a sufficient number of DCFTAs, the next move will be to adopt harmonised rules of origin permitting cumulation of value added in supply chains that involve more than two free trade partner states. The idea is to develop a regional Neighbourhood Economic Community that takes inspiration from the European Economic Area (EEA); thus a regime that facilitates increasingly deep integration of trade and investment on a regional-multilateral basis.

However this DCFTA approach, as currently proposed by the Commission, has to be taken in two stages:

o First, the 'hub-and-spoke network' of bilateral FTAs, with variable possible degrees of depth and comprehensiveness, would be extended into DCFTAs, and

o   Second, taking account of the regional-multilateral dimension, steps
would be taken to harmonise the content of the FTAs.

The DCFTA proposition raises the question what is the optimal
feasible content of the package of market integration measures. In the
extreme case, such as in the EEA with Norway, the partner states accept to
legislate and implement the entire EU single market *acquis*. The
commitment moreover is not only for the stock of EU *acquis* at the moment
of signing the treaty, but also has a continuing dynamic aspect: i.e. the
partner accepts the commitment to automatically follow all subsequent
single market measures taken by the EU. As Norway has seen with over a
decade of experience in the EEA, this dynamic aspect has been very
important, with large blocks of EU service sector regulatory policies
emerging as a second generation or wave of single market reforms since the
original 1992 programme for 'completing' the single market.

The EEA package is clearly understood to be an extreme case, which
should not be attempted by states that are still in the relatively early stages
of post-communist transition, with weak administrative and technical
capabilities to adopt such extensive commitments in the foreseeable future.
But at least this supplies a template, or reference case, by comparison with
which another template may be constructed to suit the cases of the former
Soviet states. In this respect the EU's Action Plans with each partner state
under the European Neighbourhood Policy (ENP) have been an
informative preparatory phase of work over the last three years. The
Commission's message has been that each partner state is free to choose
how far to go. However the Action Plans still follow a common and
comprehensive structure of topics. The variable then becomes how far
cooperation goes, for example in the fields of banking regulation or agri-
food standards, beyond vague declarations in favour of convergence of
standards towards legally specified and binding commitments. The ENP
Action Plans in fact largely remained at the level of vague declarations, and
it now becomes the task of the FTA (or DCFTA) negotiations to work out
what can become the subject of legally binding and operational
commitments.

Two cases, those of Ukraine and Georgia, allow us to see more clearly
where the FTA (or DCFTA) process may lead. Both countries have
comparable levels of both (positive) political commitment towards
integration with the EU, and (very limited) administrative-technical
capabilities to implement complex market regulatory policies. The striking
difference is in the level of governmental cohesion and determination to

combat corruption: Ukraine seems to be chronically incapable of forming a coherent government and does nothing to combat endemic corruption; Georgia (leaving aside here the catastrophic war with Russia in August 2008) has shown impressive coherence and determination at the economic policy level and done much to reduce corruption. These qualities (and weaknesses) link now to the FTA (and DCFTA) issues.

Ukraine advances in negotiations with the EU to agree a DCFTA as part of a new Association Agreement. The Commission has tabled a considerable list of single market *acquis* items for inclusion in the DCFTA, including industrial product standards, phyto-sanitary regulations for agricultural and agri-food products, customs code regulations, competition policy rules, government procurement, intellectual property rights and service sector liberalisation. In addition, outside there are sector-specific negotiations underway or envisaged for Ukraine to accede to the Common European Sky (civil aviation agreement) and the Energy Community Treaty (which brings the Western Balkans into the EU regulatory sphere for energy policy along with the new member states of South East Europe). Both these two last elements, for civil aviation and energy, entail commitments at the level taken on by Norway as part of the European Economic Area (EEA) in these particular sectors, i.e. taking on board whole blocks of EU single market *acquis*. It may be doubted whether Ukraine is actually capable of effectively implementing all these commitments for many years, but its overarching political priority to integrate with the EU lead it to sign up to such commitments.

Georgia by comparison has taken a different approach. Its economic strategy, which was extremely successful in overcoming the (intentionally devastating) Russian trade and economic sanctions from 2006, has been to liberalise internally and externally, de-regulate and de-corrupt the economy all in radical degrees. However Georgia was surprised to find its strategy encountering obstacles when it wanted to negotiate a fast and simple FTA with the EU. The Commission adopted the view that the DCFTA package is the only template for a useful FTA with the Eastern neighbours, and that therefore it was crucial to see whether Georgia was sufficiently committed to a substantial degree of single market *acquis* compliance. Commission officials were then somewhat shocked to hear Georgian officials (at all levels, officials, ministers, president) say that many EU regulations were not suitable for Georgia and would if seriously attempted run counter to their de-regulation and de-corruption strategy. There was then serious resistance in the Commission to the opening of FTA negotiations with Georgia, which was not overcome until after the August war when these technical objections were overruled at a higher political level.

The moral of this story of the EU's dealings with these two neighbours is that the Commission still has some institutional bias of acting as if under the paradigm of accession negotiations, even while underlining in official documents that that the ENP states have no membership perspective; i.e. using its considerable negotiating capabilities to push the neighbours far down the EU *acquis* convergence road, even when the partner state presents reasoned arguments to do less than the Commission officials recommends. This point is relevant to the purpose of the present paper, which is looking at possible means to establish overarching cooperative processes across the Eastern regions; to push for an excessive common dosage of EU *acquis* compliance can become an obstacle.

The idea of multlilateralising FTAs in the EaP region, with possible extension to Russia raises several further issues, both technical and political.

The first, following from the discussion above about Ukraine and Georgia, is how deep or simple the common FTA component should be. The answer should surely be to identify some core FTA features, especially for goods, that would maximise regional economic integration while minimising the burden of regulatory harmonisation. The minimal FTA content would consist of scrapping tariffs for goods, harmonised customs procedures and related matters (such as the TIR regime for goods in transit), and acceptance of EU-branded product standards (e.g. those carrying the CE mark). This would still leave open the possibility for the bilateral FTAs between the EU and individual partner states to take on deeper content. Therefore there could be a hybrid regime of a common FTA area combined with DCFTAs selectively according to partner state.

A key additional feature of multilaterising the FTAs would be to adopt common rules of origin to permit what is called 'diagonal cumulation'. This means a regime under which the minimum value-added required to benefit from the tariff-free advantage could be cumulated between two or more partner countries. For example a multi-stage production process might see several stages in processing from raw materials, to semi-manufactured products, and on to complex component parts and then finally finished goods. Each production stage might on its own be insufficient to meet the minimum value-added content for the free trade advantage, but when cumulated between several countries of the

FTA area it could be sufficient. The EU has seen a massive development of this kind of multinational 'supply chain' economics. The EU has also worked out with its Mediterranean free trade associated states a formal harmonised regime called the harmonised Euro-Med rules of origin. This system could be extended to an East European FTA area.

An alternative technique for achieving the same objective is to extend the EU's customs union, which already includes the non-member state Turkey. This is technically a superior and bureaucratically simpler system, since the EU's common external tariff (CET) is adopted by customs union partners. Since all imports into the customs union will have borne the CET there is no need for complicated rules of origin. However a disadvantage is that the partner states are unable to have their own preferential trade regimes with third countries. This would be an important issue as regards Russia, both if it were in or outside the FTA area. If Russia were inside the FTA area it would mean a heavy imposition of EU policies of the type that Russia objects to as a matter of political principle. If Russia were outside there would be the problem for the EaP state that had a major trading relationship and a bilateral FTA with Russia (which would have to be scrapped).

This leads finally to the major question whether Russia might be interested to join an EU-led FTA area including the EaP states, so to give real content to the idea of a Common European Economic Space. Russia has been willing to use this language in declaratory documents adopted with the EU, and the Commission speaks of the perspective of an FTA with Russia as a next step beyond Russia's WTO accession. As of today Russia is not ready politically for this. Even its WTO accession prospects are constantly being pushed back by Russian measures that would be difficult or incompatible with WTO membership – for example the sanctions against Moldova and Georgia adopted in 2006, the export duties on timber decided in principle in 2007 but currently deferred for 6 months, and most recently the substantial increase in automobile tariffs decided in November 2008 in response to the drop in oil and gas revenues.

The deeper question is whether an FTA with the EU would be in Russia's strategic economic policy interests or not, and if a positive case can be justified, how or whether the Russian policy-shaping elite might come round to this view. Russia does have the ambition to be a diversified industrial economy, rather than one massively dependent on its natural resource sectors. As of today, however, the prospects for achieving this goal are remote, as the economy has been suffering from a pronounced 'Dutch disease' effect, with the high exchange rate undermining the chances of building up a new industrial economy with international competitiveness. The policy response so far has been to intensify the state's role in the economy in order to rebuild the strength of a very widely defined set of 'strategic' enterprises and sectors. Foreign investment in Russia has been substantial, but in industrial sectors essentially devoted to import substitution, a tendency that is reinforced now by the increased import duties on automobiles.

However these tendencies should not be regarded as necessarily permanent. The present huge instability of oil prices is showing to Russia its vulnerability. It was the earlier reversal of the first 1973 oil shock that is seen as having played a significant role in the economic and political collapse of the Soviet Union. The now-weakening rouble exchange rate may alleviate the concern for cost competitiveness. More fundamentally the Russian leadership may come to appreciate the need for deeper integration with the European economy as a necessary part of its industrial strategy. Russia looks today at both China and the EU as its major economic partners. Russian political leaders may stress the Eurasian dimension in speeches to counter European pressures on political topics such as democracy; but as economic partner Russia is literally terrified at the prospect of being overwhelmed by China in any economic sector, and geographically in the Far East region in particular. On this comparison one can sense that while an FTA between Russia and China is virtually inconceivable, an FTA with the EU is a relatively attractive proposition. Russia has already experience of very extensive business relationships with Europe, first of all with Germany but also with virtually every EU member state. The idea of balanced partnerships is more plausible. On top of this there may in due course be a swing in the centre of gravity in the thinking and analysis of Russian policy-making circles and business interests in favour of internationally competitive 'supply chain' economics, rather than more isolationist-nationalist policies. There is a debate in Russia on the choice between these two tendencies – the internationalist modernisers versus the nationalist isolationists. For the time being the latter have the edge, but circumstances and learning experiences may change this in due course. A contributing factor from the EU side could be success in developing its FTA area with the EaP states; if this becomes a tangible prospect or reality Russia may become extremely concerned about its exclusion.

If the idea of the EaP regional FTA begins to take shape, a natural question will be a possible link to the existing Euro-Med free trade area. The same logic as that discussed above, that of bilateral FTAs being combined with a regional multilateral element with common rules of origin, already exists in the Mediterranean region. The EU has bilateral FTAs with virtually all Med states, and moves ahead with a regional-multilateral regime with the most advanced 'Agadir group' (Morocco, Tunisia, Egypt, Jordan) which have agreed to the 'Pan-Euro-Med' rules of origin. The scenario could therefore be to create a mega pan-Euro-Med FTA with all the neighbourhood countries of East and South that had bilateral FTAs with the EU and had agreed the common rules of origin regime.

Finally, the last conceivable extension of this scenario would be to include Central Asia in a grand pan-Eurasian-Med FTA area. There is already the CIS-sponsored matrix of bilateral FTAs, including almost all Central Asian countries. If Russia were to join the EaP FTA area, there could be a movement of interest among the Central Asian states to join in as well. This is of course the most remote prospect as of now. Key to whether this would remain just a theoretical possibility is Kazakhstan, which wishes to give substance to its new 'Path to Europe' and already shares with Russia membership of their Eurasian Economic Area. The idea might be discussed in speeches and seminars, to at least open up mental horizons and test reactions.

Conclusion: The idea of a Pan-European Economic Space is a first candidate for consideration, because it could be based on existing EU competences and the current momentum in extension of the EU's network of regional free trade agreements. Negotiations for Deep Free Trade Agreements (DFTAs) are underway or envisaged for the Eastern partners, and the mechanism of harmonised pan-Euro-Mediterranean rules of origin exists and can be extended in application with a view to a wider pan-European (or Euro-Med) regional-multilateral free trade area. In addition the Commission expresses its interest in an FTA with Russia. But here there is still a blockage, first with Russia's failure yet to join the WTO, but also with more fundamental opposition within Russia to an FTA with the EU, which some consider to be advantageous mainly for the EU. The current global recession intensifies Russian protectionism (e.g. already for cars). The counterargument is that Russia's economic policy is failing to develop a diversified and competitive industrial economy, and that at some point trade liberalisation with the EU will have to be part of the remedial therapy.

5. TRANSPORT NETWORKS

The planning and implementation of pan-European transport networks fits naturally into the logic of the present study.

Early work on pan-European transport issues in the 1980s was led by the UN Economic Commission for Europe (UNECE). However in the 1990s, with the introduction of the Trans-European Network (TEN) concept in the Maastricht Treaty, the European Community became the leading actor. The EU adopted 30 priority projects for road and rail corridors, which will take until 2020 to be completed and are receiving massive financing from national and EU (Commission, European Investment Bank) sources, with €126 billion of investments up to 2007, another €150 billion until 2013, and a further €120 billion by 2020.[11] These investments mainly concern the enlarged EU of 27 member states.

However at the same time there has been ambitious planning work done at the pan-European level, extending these networks into the former Soviet Union. An overall concept was established at a first conference of transport ministers in Prague in 1991. At their second conference in Crete in 1994 ministers defined ten priority pan-European transport corridors as routes in Central and Eastern Europe that required major investment over the following ten to fifteen years. Additions were made at the third conference in Helsinki in 1997. These corridors are distinct from the Trans-European transport networks within the European Union, although there are proposals to combine the two systems.

The pan-European corridors that link the EU to Russia, Belarus and Ukraine are the following:

o *Corridor II:* Road and rail link connecting Berlin–Warsaw–Minsk-Moscow-Nizhny Novgorod. Major investments have been made in the Polish segment. Rehabilitation and upgrading of motorway in the

---

[11] European Commission, "TEN-T – Trans-European Transport Projects – Implementation of the Priority Projects Progress Report", May 2008.

Belarus and Russian segments are needed, together with technical modernisation and administrative improvements of border crossings, which still suffer long delays.

o *Corridor III:* Road and rail connection between Dresden–Wroclaw–L'viv–Kiev. The Ukrainian road segments (2 lane highways) do not yet meet European standards, and the delays at border crossings into Ukraine are substantial (4-5 hours). Some European Bank for Reconstruction and Development (EBRD) funding is being made available.

o *Corridor V:* Road and rail connections between Venice–Trieste–Koper–Ljubljana–Budapest–Uzgorod–L'viv. The Ukrainian segment achieves limited success so far, helped however by some EBRD investments.

o *Corridor IX:* Road and rail connection between Helsinki–St. Petersburg–Pskov/Moscow–Kiev–Ljubasevka–Chisinau–Bucharest–Dimitrovgrad–Alexandroupolis. Improvements have been made in infrastructure, but administrative problems at border crossings remain the major hindrances to road and rail traffic along this corridor.[12]

Following the strong development of the TEN networks in the enlarged EU it was decided in 2004 to create a high-level group to prepare plans to extend these to neighbouring countries and regions. This High Level (Palacio) Group, brought together the EU member states, 26 neighbouring countries through to Central Asia and the international financial institutions (IFIs) to plan a set of trans-European transport axes. Its report of November 2005[13] identified five such axes, four of which are relevant to the present study:

o *Motorways of the seas,* including the Black Sea and Caspian Sea. This would consist of 14 priority projects, including investments at the

---

[12] For a comprehensive report on the ten Pan-European corridors, see "PAN-EUROSTAR - Pan-European Transport Corridors and Areas Status Report", Final Report, November 2005.

[13] European Commission, "Networks for Peace and Development – Extension of the major trans-European transport axes to the neighbouring countries and regions", Report of the High Level Group chaired by Loyala de Palacio, November 2005.

Russian ports of St. Petersberg, Ust-Luga and Novorossisk, and Illyiehevsk (Ukraine), Poti (Georgia) and Baku (Azerbaijan).

o *Northern axis*, joining the EU with the Norwegian/Russian Barents region.

o *Central axis*, from the EU through Ukraine to the Caucasus and Central Asia, with connections also to the Volga River basin and the Trans-Siberian railway. Overall 19 road, rail and multi-modal projects were identified, mostly falling in Russia and Ukraine, and including a high-speed railway connection between St. Petersberg and Moscow, improved connections with the trans-Siberian railway, upgrading of main highways in Ukraine, and other fundamental infrastructures.

o *South-eastern axis*, from the EU through the Balkans and Turkey through to the Caucasus and Caspian regions and connections with Russia. This would consist of 46 priority projects, mostly located in South-East Europe, with extensions through Turkey into the South Caucasus and Middle East.

The total cost of the projects identified to support the fives axes of the Palacio report was estimated at €45 billion, of which €35 billion would be invested until 2020.

The EU has in addition developed an ambitious programme for southern transport routes from the EU through the Black Sea and Caspian Sea region into Central Asia. This TRACECA (Transport Corridor Europe-Caucasus-Asia) initiative was established in a multilateral agreement signed in 1998, and aimed at improving road, rail and maritime transport networks linking 14 states of the East European, Caucasian and Central Asian region (Armenia, Azerbaijan, Bulgaria, Georgia, Kazakhstan, Kyrgyzstan, Moldova, Romania, Tajikistan, Turkey, Turkmenistan, Ukraine and Uzbekistan). TRACECA's initiating conference was subtitled Restoration of the Historic Silk Route, thus suggesting a high level of ambition. Since 2001 it has a permanent secretariat based in Baku. It thus works on southern routes without Russia. TRACECA has developed a large agenda of projects to support identified transport routes, as well as efforts at reform and convergence of legal and regulatory regimes.

Notwithstanding its ambitious objectives the TRACECA initiative is generally considered to be rather unsuccessful. The reasons for this seem to be the weak inclination of the Central Asian governments to enter into cooperative relations with their neighbours, the limitation of the EU's contribution to mainly technical assistance, without strong investment financing, and the weakness of the permanent secretariat in Baku.

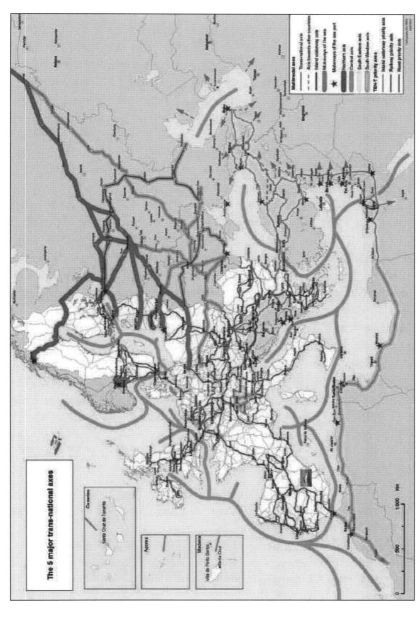

Source: European Commission, "Networks for Peace and Development – Extension of the major trans-European transport axes to the neighbouring countries and regions", Report of the High Level Group chaired by Loyala de Palacio, November 2005.

The Northern Dimension programme, initiated in 1998 under Finnish leadership, and renewed in 2007 in a new format bringing together the EU, Iceland, Norway and Russia, has seen perhaps the most advanced efforts to extend the transnational corridors and axes beyond the EU's territory.[14] This reflects the relatively compact geographic area under consideration, the technical-diplomatic competence and focus of the Finnish and Norwegian diplomats and experts driving the programme, coupled with the resources of the European Union. Since a large part of EU-Russian trade passes through Baltic sea ports and road and rail links to Finland and the Baltic states, in principle the EU and Russia share the same objective of providing an efficient transport infrastructure to service this trade. However Russia has moved away from the idea of 'Pan-European' networks, in favour of 'Russia's international transport connections'. This difference of language is reflected concretely in Russia's drive to develop its own port facilities in North-West Europe, for example with new ports such as Ust-Luga and Primorsk intended to displace the existing ports of Baltic Sea states and Finland, as well as Gazprom's drive together with German business interests to build the Nord Stream pipeline direct to Germany, by-passing the transit countries of land routes. The development plan of Russian railways is coordinated with these port developments. Russia also seeks to develop its own transit role to the East, seeking to be the transport bridge for Chinese and other Far East trade with Europe, including by air flights overflying Siberia.[15] In addition Russia's domestic infrastructures are in bad need of rehabilitation at huge cost: the railway development plan calls for €360 billion of investments until 2030, whereas the transport system as a whole calls for investments of €583 billion until 2015.[16]

---

[14] *The New Northern Dimension*, op. cit. See in particular the chapter by Katri Pynnoniemi, "EU-Russian cooperation on transport: Prospects for the Northern Dimension Transport Partnership".

[15] The Siberian overflying fees, amounting to €330 million in 2005, remains a long-standing subject of contention between the EU and Russia. The EU regards these fees as contravening the 1944 Chicago Convention on International Civil Aviation. In 2007 there was a further row over Russian pressure on Lufthansa to move its regional cargo hub from Astana in Kazakhstan to Krasnoyarsk in Russia.

[16] K. Pynnoniemi, op. cit.

While Russia has thus been prioritising the development of new infrastructures and renewing old ones, the EU has been more concerned over the inefficiencies (long delays, obsolete administrative procedures, and corruption) at border crossings into Russia from Finland, Belarus and Ukraine. These issues are at least being addressed in working group meetings between the EU and Russia, both in the regional framework of the Northern Dimension and in the wider framework of the EU-Russia 'common spaces'. The latter EU-Russia activity consists of a 'dialogues' in five working groups, for air, maritime, inland waterway, road and rail transport.

In spite of these various difficulties it was agreed in October 2008 by the Northern Dimension partners to engage in more strongly structured cooperation in the transport domain through setting up a Northern Dimension Partnership on Transport and Logistics. This will be established during 2009 and become fully operational on 1 January 2010. This will be a jointly agreed programme covering all modes of transport, with a focus on both infrastructural and non-infrastructural sources of bottlenecks. There will be a three-level institutional set-up, with high-level ministerial meetings, a steering group of senior officials and a permanent secretariat. Several IFIs are invited to collaborate – the Nordic Investment Bank (NIB), the EBRD, EIB and World Bank. Notably relevant for the present study, Belarus is invited to join the Partnership, given its importance for road, rail and energy pipeline transit.

It is a matter for consideration whether this Partnership model might be extended to other regions of the wider European neighbourhood. There would be two main candidates for such an approach: the central axis with the transit role of Ukraine, and the south-eastern axis going beyond south-east Europe through to Central Asia and the Far East. For the central axis both Ukraine and Moldova are open to adopting elements of the EU's transport *acquis*, unlike Russia. This regulatory approximation would therefore be organised on a bilateral basis with these countries, leaving the possible Partnership to deal with other infrastructure matters. To the East the strategic question for the EU is how to develop both of two routes to the north and south of the Black Sea. The TRACECA project favours the southern route to the exclusion of Russia.

Extending further east, there are also Joint Ministerial meetings of the Euro-Asian Transport Conference, the 4th held in Warsaw in June 2007, which aims at promoting road transport connections between South-East

Asia, China and Europe. The World Congress of the International Road Transport Union in Istanbul in May 2008, held under the title The Revival of the Silk Road, launched the New Eurasian Land Transport Initiative (NELTI), identifying three routes:

o   Northern, from Moscow through Kazakhstan into China;

o   Central, from South East Europe across the Black Sea-Caucasus-Caspian Sea through Turkmenistan, Uzbekistan and Kazakhstan into China, and

o   Southern, from Turkey through Iran, Turkmenistan, Uzbekistan and Kazakhstan into China.

The Asian Development Bank (ADB) and China are keen to develop the land routes between the EU and China transiting Central Asia. Since 1997 the ADB has been promoting the Central Asia Regional Economic Cooperation (CAREC) programme, which brings together all Central Asian states (except Turkmenistan), Afghanistan, Azerbaijan, China and Mongolia. In November 2008 the ADB announced a $700 million loan to improve a segment of the central route through Kazakhstan, as part of an ambitious $6.7 billion programme to be completed by 2015. Especially interesting from a European standpoint is the CAREC programme for regulatory harmonisation and simplification, which seeks to find a rational way ahead amidst the conflicting standards of the former Soviet Union, China and the EU.[17] The CAREC policy roadmap in fact recommends a significant convergence on EU standards for road vehicles and emissions, and for cross-border transport user charges. There is therefore a natural partnership to be developed between the EU and its TRACECA programme and CAREC. On funding on the European side the EBRD is already fully mandated to work on transport infrastructures, and the European Investment Bank received at the end of 2008 a mandate to extend its operations beyond East Europe and Russia into central Asia. The ENPI now has a grant investment facility which can be usefully combined with equity and loan investment funds from the EBRD and EIB, but again there is at present a limitation of these ENPI funds to the Eastern Partnership states.

---

[17] Asian Development Bank, "Central Asia Regional Economic Cooperation: Harmonisation and Simplification of Transport Agreements, Cross-Border Documents and Transport Regulations", Staff Consultant's report, October 2005.

Transcontinental Railway and Road Corridors Connecting the CAREC Member Countries with the Rest of the World

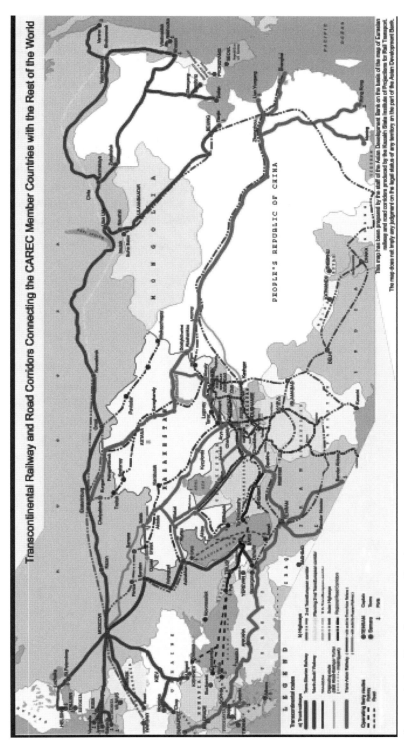

Source: Asian Development Bank.

Conclusion: The pan-European transport infrastructures and networks has been the subject of intensive planning work for almost two decades, with the successful (consensual) identification of priority axes or corridors. At the level of implementation relatively large sums are being invested by the EU institutions and national governments in the intra-EU networks. Their extension beyond the EU into Eastern Europe and Central Asia progresses much less fast, due not only to lesser access to funding, but also to bureaucratic and political obstacles. A new development is the interest coming from East Asia in developing the major Eurasian land connections, with projects leading into Central Asia supported by the Asian Development Bank: these could be linked up with EU-supported projects. The opening of a mandate for the EIB to operate in Central Asia in co-financing operations with the EBRD could link up with ADB-funded Eurasian transport corridors.

6. Energy

The main gas pipelines, actual and projected, connecting the EU with Russia and Central Asia with various possible transit routes through Eastern and South-Eastern Europe, highlight different paradigms: of strategic cooperation and solidarity *versus* competition and differentiated risk exposure. These issues were dramatically amplified by the January 2009 crisis with the cutting of supplies through Ukraine to Europe for two weeks, with serious damage suffered immediately by Slovakia and Bulgaria. The responsibility for the stoppage is contested between Russia and Ukraine, while the President of the Commission blamed both parties.

The strategic pipeline options are well identified: the actual Ukraine and Belarus transit routes, and the planned Nord Stream, South Stream, Nabucco and Southern Corridor projects.

Ukraine's gas transportation system (GTS)

Ukraine's GTS currently transports 80% of Russian gas supplies to Europe. The capacity of the trunk gas transit pipeline is currently around 120 billion cubic meters, exceeding the capacity of all bypassing projects taken together. Since the early 1990s, Ukrainian-Russian relations in the energy sphere have been volatile and disruptive. On 1 January 2006 Gazprom interrupted the gas supply to Ukraine following their disagreement over a gas price. In response, Ukraine started to withdraw gas from the transit pipeline. The crisis acquired a European dimension, after several European states did not receive their gas in full. The new crisis three years later, in January 2009, followed the same sequence: deadlocked negotiations over price, then supply interruption, then a compromise agreement on price and supply resumption.

Moreover, the technical state of Ukraine's GTS is of great concern. Most of the pipelines were built in the period from 1960 to 1980 and since the collapse of the USSR have not undergone comprehensive checks and repairs. Already in 2004 an expert study indicated that 20% of the pipelines exceeded their life span. This increases the risk of a technical breakdown causing a disruption of supplies to the EU. In 2007 an EU-commissioned study determined that €2.5 billion would be needed to rehabilitate the GTS. Due to defective economic governance, Naftogaz – a state energy company, which operates the pipeline – has often been in debt-default and is unable to ensure such investments. The European Commission and Ukraine co-organised a conference in March 2009 to address the financing of repair work.

Countries affected by the January 2009 gas crisis

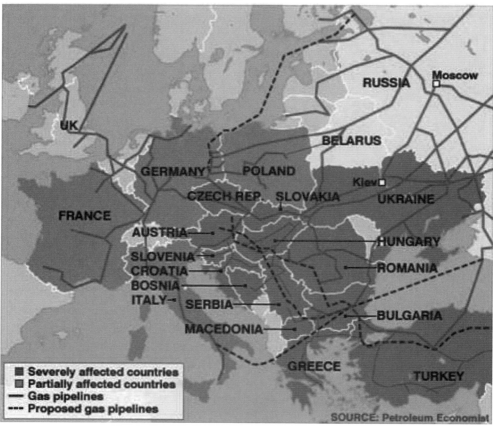

Source: BBC (http://news.bbc.co.uk/2/hi/europe/7830517.stm).

Yamal-Europe pipeline

The Yamal-Europe pipeline was built in 1999 with a view of avoiding Ukraine and transporting Russian gas through Belarus and Poland to Germany. According to the initial design, there should have been two lines of the pipeline – with a yearly capacity of 65 billion cubic meters (bcm) of gas – running along each other. Only the first line – currently transporting around 33 bcm – has been built so far. The Polish section is managed by a private company, Europol Gaz, 48% of which belongs to Gazprom and another 48% to PGNiG, a Polish state energy company. The Belarusian section is managed by a state energy company Beltransgaz. In 2007 Belarus pledged to sell a 50% stake in Beltransgaz to Gazprom by 2011 in exchange for a gradual rising of the gas price to the European level. Already in 2000 Gazprom renounced its plans to build the second line of the Yamal-Europe pipeline, despite its relatively cheap cost, since the first pipeline was laid down with a view of fitting the second line. Gazprom's decision has been motivated by the desire to completely avoid the transit states, notably through the Nord Stream project economic costs.

Nord Stream

The Nord Stream pipeline, planned since 2000, is intended to run offshore from Vyborg in Russia to Greisfwald in Germany. The first line – with a capacity of 25 bcm of gas per year – is planned to be operating by 2011, but this timetable seems likely to slip by a few years. The project is still undergoing environmental assessments with Baltic states expressing concern. The pipeline would be supplied with gas coming from the Shtockman gas field, planned to be put in operation by Gazprom (with Total and StatoilHydro as its partners) by the time Nord Stream is ready. The estimated costs of the pipeline are around €7.4 billion. It is to be owned and built by a consortium, including Gazprom (51%), E.ON Ruhrgas (20%), BASF (20%), and Gasunie (9%). No pipes have yet been laid in the Baltic Sea, but large quantities of pipes have been contracted for about €500 million, and are being supplied and stocked near St. Petersberg.

South Stream

This proposed gas pipeline was initially planned to transport 30 bcm of Russian natural gas across the Black Sea to be landed in Bulgaria, but the latest statements from Gazprom cite 47 bcm. The offshore section crosses the Black Sea from the Russian coast at Beregovaya (where also the Blue Stream pipeline originates) to Varna on the Bulgarian coast for a total of 900 kilometres through Ukrainian waters at maximum depths of 2,000 meters.[18] The project began to advance in June 2007, with the signing of a Memorandum of Understanding by Gazprom and Eni.[19] Then, in January 2008, the two companies created a joint venture, South Stream AG, equally owned by the two companies. A feasibility study is expected to be completed by Saipem, a subsidiary of Eni, by the end of 2009.[20] The latest Gazprom statements indicate that a more southerly route through Turkish waters is now being considered. At the same time the estimated cost is said to have doubled over the latest year, to reach €19-24 billion.[21]

South Stream has two possible routes, the first heading south-west through Greece and Albania and then crossing the Adriatic Sea to join the Italian network, and the second heading north-west crossing Serbia and Hungary on into Central Europe, and linking the other gas pipelines from Russia. The project is planned to become operational in 2012. The consortium needs to make agreements with the transit countries, and Russia has been doing this with agreements concluded with Bulgaria, Serbia, Hungary and Greece.[22] In general, the project has been welcomed by transit countries, but is contested by Ukraine, through whose maritime shelf it has to pass.[23] Although Ukraine's power to ban the project is in doubt, some speculate that Ukraine will permit the construction of South Stream in exchange for the Russian permit to build the White Stream offshore gas pipeline from Georgia to Ukraine. Also, Gazprom has not been able to find an agreement with Austria (which instead supports the rival Nabucco project) leading to a re-thinking of the north-bound route which may instead pass through Slovenia.

---

[18] *The South Stream Project*, Eni and Gazprom, 23 June 2007, Rome.

[19] Eni, "Gazprom set up company for South Stream gas pipelines", Forbes.com, 18 January 2008 (http://www.forbes.com/feeds/afx/2008/01/18/afx4548113.html).

[20] *Gazprom's plans for South Stream gas pipeline become more ambitious*, Businessneseurope, 13 February 2009 (http://businessneweurope.eu/story1451/Gazproms_plans_for_South_Stream_gas_pipeline_become_more_ambitious).

[21] *South Stream to boost Europe's energy security*, 10 February 2009, RIA NOVOSTI.

[22] *South Stream to boost Europe's energy security*, RIA Novosti, 10 February 2009 (http://en.rian.ru/analysis/20090210/120071766.html).

[23] Stanimir Vaglenov, *South Stream Turns into Southern Dream*, 9 December 2008, Varna.

Possible routes of proposed gas pipelines

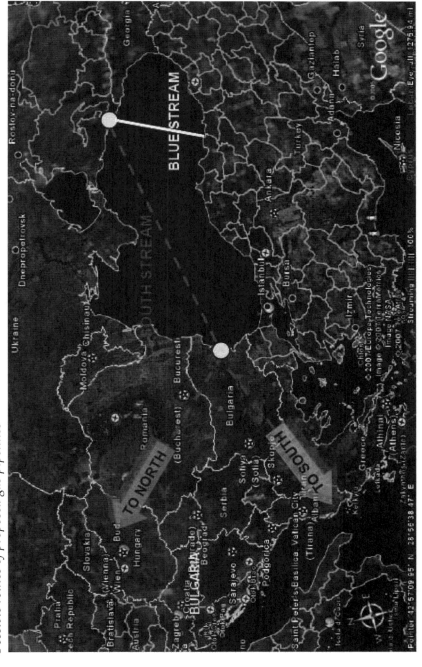

Source: Eni.

Nabucco

The planned Nabucco pipeline would transport natural gas from Turkey to Austria, via Bulgaria, Romania and Hungary. It will run from Erzurum in Turkey to Baumgarten an der March, a major natural gas hub in Austria. Its total length is expected to be 3,300 kilometres and its estimated cost is around €7.9 billion. The initial deliveries are expected to be between 4.5 and 13 billion cubic meters per annum, of which 2 to 8 bcm would go to Baumgarten. By 2020, the transmission volume is expected to reach 31 bcm per annum, of which up to 16 bcm would go to Baumgarten. The project is backed by the European Union and the United States.

Nabucco pipeline route

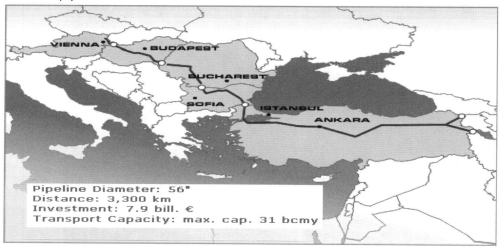

The adequacy of gas supplies to fill the Nabucco-pipeline is the subject of continuing debate. Different supply sources discussed include:

o   Azerbaijan. The Shah Deniz gas fields should come onstream in 2013 (8 bcm)

o   Turkmenistan. It could possibly supply around 10 bcm if the Trans-Caspian gas pipeline would be built.

o   Iran. This option is for the time being rejected by the US and the EU.

o   Kazakhstan. It has huge reserves and could in principle provide gas through the planned trans-Caspian gas pipeline if the latter would be built.

o   Egypt. Their new gas discoveries might feed Nabucco through the Arab Gas Pipeline but the increase in domestic demand may limit Egypt's' exports.

o   Iraq. This option seems not to be considered now.

o   Russia. Its gas could feed Nabucco through the Blue Stream pipeline.

Six companies are currently involved in the project: OMV of Austria, MOL of Hungary, Bulgargaz of Bulgaria, the German RWE (since February 2008), Transgaz of Romania and BOTAŞ of Turkey. Each of them owns 16.67% of the shares. The talks on the project first started in February 2002 and, in June 2002, five companies signed a protocol of intention to construct it, followed by a Cooperation Agreement in October 2002. The project was confirmed at the political level at a summit meeting in Budapest on 27 January 2009 attended by the consortium partners (Austria, Bulgaria, Germany, Romania and Turkey), potential suppliers (Azerbaijan, Egypt, Iraq and Turkmenistan) and transit country Georgia, the European Commission and the current Czech Presidency.

Southern corridor

The Nabucco project also leads on to related initiatives to pipe gas across the Caspian from Turkmenistan. At the Nabucco summit on 26-27 January 2009, the communiqué welcomed the Commission's initiative to establish a Caspian Development Corporation (CDC) and a Caspian Energy Company (CEC), launched by the Austrian OMV company and the German RWE. These initiatives are intended to assure the supply of Turkmen gas into Nabucco, the prospects for which have been improving with better relations between Azerbaijan and Turkmenistan, and a recent report (from a European consultancy) of greatly increased reserves in Turkmenistan. These developments open the prospect of being able to reconcile Turkmenistan's existing commitments to supply large quantities to Russia (for onward sale to the EU) with a trans-Caspian pipeline to Baku (securing the viability of Nabucco) as well as a pipeline to China.

Gazprom's financial constraints

Gazprom is hard hit by the global economic and financial crisis. The demand for Russian gas from Europe in November 2008 fell by 24% in comparison to October, and the price for European importers is expected to fall, following the oil price, from $400-500 per thousand m3 to $250-280 in the course of 2009. As a result, Gazprom's export revenues are expected to fall by 31.7%, or \$20 billion, in 2009.[24] Gazprom's plans to compensate for its future losses by raising internal gas prices also seem increasingly unrealistic, given the tense social situation. As a result Gazprom might have limited access to Western credit, which might have an adverse affect on the Nord Stream project, as 70% of its costs are planned to be covered with borrowings from the international market, and even more so the less advanced South Stream project.[25] It might make Gazprom and its European partners look for more economical solutions.

A gas transit consortium in Ukraine

An international gas transit consortium – bringing Ukraine, the EU and Russia to jointly manage the Ukrainian trunk gas pipeline – could in this situation provide a solution, addressing the energy security challenges of Russia as a supplier, Ukraine for its transit role and the EU as consumer. An attempt to establish such a consortium was undertaken in 2002, but failed to reach agreement.[26] In 2004 the parties returned to the status quo, which has proved so defective.

Three types of arrangement for a consortium could be considered: privatisation and sale, a concession under a long-term lease or a management contract. Currently, the privatisation of the GTS is prohibited by a law "On Pipelines" that was almost unanimously voted in by the Ukrainian parliament in February 2007. On the other hand, a management contract would leave the need to finance major investments in rehabilitation of the GTS with the Ukrainian government. As the middle way, a concession of the major trunk pipeline trunk for a period of between 25 to 50 years would seem the best solution for all parties.

---

[24] "Gazprom poteriaet v Evrope \$20 milliardov", *Kommersant*, 15 December 2008 (http://www.kommersant.ru/doc.aspx?DocsID=1094437).

[25] "Prositsia v trubu", *Vedomosti* 23 December 2008 (http://www.vedomosti.ru/newspaper/article.shtml?2008/12/23/174909).

[26] A possibility to establish an international gas transportation consortium has been evaluated by Razumkov Centre, *Gas Transportation Consortium*, National Security and Defense Magazine, No. 1, 2004 (http://www.uceps.org/files/category_journal/NSD49_eng.pdf) and World Bank, *Ukraine: Challenges facing the gas sector*, 2003. For a detailed investigation of the consortium negotiations, see Elena Gnedina, "Ukraine's Pipeline Politics", *Europe-Asia Studies*, forthcoming.

Due to the high sensitivity of the subject, consortium negotiations would need to be conducted at both corporate and political levels. The corporate negotiations should be conducted by Gazprom, Naftohaz, one or more European energy companies and the EBRD. The European participation might be selected on the basis of an open competition (in the past Ruhrgas, Gaz de France, ENI and Shell demonstrated interest in participating). The consortium would take the form of a public-private partnership, and could also secure substantial funding from the participating governments, the European Commission, the EBRD, EIB and the World Bank. The EBRD in particular is able to take an equity share participation in such projects. The EIB and World Bank could supply substantial loan capital. The division of shareholdings between participants could take many different formulas in the detail. However from a strategic point of view it would seem plausible that neither the EU, Russian nor Ukrainian party would have a dominant position, for example 30% each with a remaining 10% taken up by the EBRD. The role of the EBRD could be particularly valuable, since its professional task would be to assure the correct corporate governance of the consortium.

The EU, Russia and Ukraine would provide the political guarantees. In addition to an agreement between consortium participants there should be a binding Treaty establishing the ground rules, signed and ratified by the EU, and Russian and Ukrainian governments. The treaty would inter alia protect the consortium from political instability and establish the highest-level legal basis for its operations. In particular it should specify how the trunk pipeline of the consortium would be legally and managerially separate from the domestic Ukrainian gas distribution network. It should further guarantee the ground rules for the setting of transit fees, which would be the secure revenue base of the consortium, and hence a bankable basis upon which to raise funding for renewal and repair of the pipeline.

There are indications that Moscow remains interested in the consortium idea, with recent speeches to this effect by both Medvedev and Putin.[27]

---

[27] See Medvedev's speech, Germany, 5 June 2008 at http://www.kremlin.ru/appears/2008/06/05/1923_type63374type63376type63377_202133.shtml.

Discussion of alternative scenarios

The proposed reconfiguration of the Ukrainian trunk pipeline, if it could be made to work correctly, would clearly be the most economical option, costing only about €2 billion of rehabilitation costs. Its political implications for tripartite cooperation on such an important matter would also be exactly in line with the strategic idea underlying the present study. The South Stream project, especially if added to a rehabilitated Ukrainian pipeline and Nord Stream, would be very costly and probably beyond Russia's supply potential. The Nabucco pipeline is desirable as an instrument of supply diversification and security, and its supply prospects, while still uncertain, seem to be improving especially with the other Southern Corridor initiatives. Nabucco could still become a cooperative venture with both Russia and Central Asian states as well as South East Europe, since Russian gas could enter it via the Blue Stream pipeline across the Black Sea into Turkey. One could also envisage a partial merger of the Nabucco and South Stream projects on land west of Bulgaria: i.e. if Gazprom was able to fund and supply the South Stream across the Black Sea it might make a cooperation agreement to share the on-land pipelines to be laid across South East Europe.

The EU's gas supply security would of course also be greatly improved by internal EU measures along the lines already proposed by the Commission (internal gas network connections for Baltic and South East European countries, internal gas market integration, network connections to the growing capacity of LNG import terminals).

Conclusion: For the purpose of the present study, seeking synergies from cooperative projects between the EU, Russia, Eastern Europe and Central Asia, the gas pipeline network options are of inescapable importance. There are now five major pipelines, actual or planned, that come into play: the two main land routes from Russia transiting through Ukraine and Belarus, the Nord and South Stream projects that would avoid transit countries before reaching the EU, and the Nabucco/Southern Corridor being promoted by the EU. Of these a reconfiguration of the Ukrainian trunk pipeline, with a long-term concession leased to a tripartite (EU-RUS-UKR) consortium supported by a tri-partite Treaty, could offer outstanding economic and political benefits. The Nabucco/Southern Corridor plans also open up tripartite (EU, Eastern Europe, Central Asia) cooperative possibilities, which could conceivably become quadripartite if Russia accepted the offer to join in too.

7. THE WATER-ENERGY-FOOD NEXUS IN CENTRAL ASIA

In Central Asia there is a need to address the major crisis in the regional hydroenergy-water–food nexus, with Kyrgyzstan and Tajikistan unable to develop their full hydro-electric potential sufficiently for their own energy needs, while their limited release of waters for irrigating agriculture in the three downstream countries results in food shortage crises, especially in Uzbekistan and Turkmenistan.[28] The result is already seen in humanitarian distress through lack of heating and/or food, and threatens to provoke inter-state conflicts. The ecological disaster of the Aral Sea is a further result of the gross mismanagement of water resources, starting in the Soviet period.

The water resources of Central Asia, and the Aral Sea basin in particular, flow from two major river basins, the Syr-Darya and Amu-Darya, most of whose waters originate in Kyrgyzstan and Tajikistan, respectively. Most of these water resources end up being used for irrigating the agriculture of downstream Kazakhstan, Turkmenistan and Uzbekistan. The demand for water has exceeded supply for many years. However this water deficit is certain to worsen with fast-growing populations, industrial development and the expansion of irrigated land. Moreover global warming is rapidly shrinking the water reserves in the glaciers of the Pamir and Alay mountains; these decreased by 25% between 1957 and 2000, and are expected to decline a further 25% by 2025. These problems are further exacerbated by the seasonal conflicts of interest, between the upstream

---

[28] For detailed accounts see Eurasian Development Bank, "EDB Eurasian Integration Yearbook, 2008", Almaty; and in particular a study of the EBD Strategy and Research Department, "Water and Energy Resources in Central Asia: Development and Utilisation Issues"; and UNDP, Regional Office for Europe and the CIS, "Central Asia Regional Risk Assessment: Responding to Water, Energy, and Food Security", January 2009.

states wishing to maximise their winter off-take of water to generate hydro electricity, whereas the downstream states need the water in the summer. As the competitive struggle for water resources becomes increasingly severe, political strains rise, with correspondingly growing chances of open conflict. Low-level conflict can easily arise since the downstream countries control vital transport routes into the upstream states. The Uzbek-Tajik relationship has shown continuous tensions.

Water management in Central Asia: state and impact

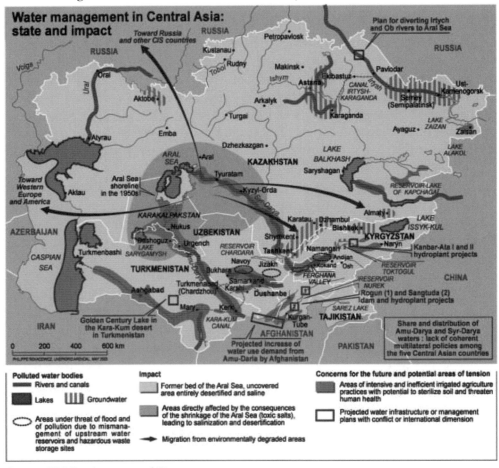

Source: UN Environmental Programme.

   In Soviet times the water discharge was maximised during summer times for irrigational use. Following independence downstream states stopped supplying Kyrgyzstan with fuel and electricity during the winter, and as a result Kyrgyzstan massively shifted its seasonal pattern of water discharge from summer to winter, thus causing catastrophic difficulties downstream (in 1995-2007 it discharged 2.5 times as much in winter as in 1985-1991, whereas in the summer it discharged in 1995-2007 two-thirds of the amount during 1985-1991).

Both Tajikistan and Kyrgyzstan wish to develop their hydro-electric power sectors. UN sources estimate that Tajikistan is only using 5%, and Kyrgyzstan 14% of their hydro-electric potential. The biggest hydro power plants planned are at Rogun in Tajikistan and Kambarata in Kyrgyzstan, both of which would cost around $2-3 billion. An uncoordinated exploitation of these expanded hydroelectric facilities would risk further aggravating the problems in downstream states of winter flooding and summer shortages. The Russian aluminium company RUSAL was planning to be the lead investor in the Rogun project but has withdrawn in favour of smaller projects. The main Russian electricity enterprise, RAO UES, has extensive interests in Kyrgyz and Tajik electricity networks, and will surely wish to play a leading role there, but they cannot alone manage the entire challenge. However the major IFIs here, the World Bank and Asian Development Bank, have a policy not to invest in major hydro power plants unless adequate consultative procedures with downstream states and ecological impact assessments have been satisfactorily completed. They have not participated in new hydro installations in the last 15 years.

A systematization of international law in this field was assembled first in the 1966 Treaty on The Helsinki Rules for the utilization of the waters of international rivers, which set out the principle of 'reasonable and fair use' of such waters and refuted the idea of unrestricted territorial sovereignty over trans-border rivers. These Helsinki Rules however are only recommendations, and it took until 1997 for the UN General Assembly to approve what could become a legally binding instrument, the Convention on the Law of Non-Navigational Utilisation of International Rivers. But the Convention had been signed by only 16 states and ratified by only 9, and is unlikely to come into force in the near future. Other elements of international law include the EU's framework Water Directive, which is an example of highly operational legislation, but of course it has jurisdiction only within the EU.

The states of Central Asia have signed many multilateral regional agreements on water usage since the beginning of the post-Soviet period, starting in 1992 with the Cooperation Agreement on the Joint Regulation,

Utilisation and Protection of Water Resources from Inter-State Sources. However most of these texts, including various bilateral agreements, have not been implemented, although they may have served to prevent the outbreak of open conflict and responded to short-term crisis situations. In October 2008 there was a short-term agreement made by all five Central Asian states under which Kazakhstan would supply electricity and coal to Kyrgyzstan (and further agreed to provide financial assistance in December), Uzbekistan would supply electricity to both Kyrgyzstan and Tajikistan, and Turkmenistan would supply electricity via Uzbekistan. In return Kyrgyzstan committed itself to release specified quantities of water to Uzbekistan for irrigation early in the vegetative period in 2009. Electricity supplies for Turkmenistan increased substantially in the last quarter of 2008, but then the curse of non-cooperation struck again. Tensions remain between Tajikistan and Uzbekistan over the former's plans to expand the Rogun dam, the agreement over the transiting of Turkmen electricity through Uzbekistan to Tajikistan broke down, and latest information is that these supplies were stopped in January 2009.[29]

The challenge therefore remains of working out a complex multinational cooperation agreement and financing major investments. There have been several attempts already to design a strategy by the World Bank, the US and an EU technical assistance project. Such a strategy would require large commitments by the World Bank and other IFIs, and the willingness of Russia to cooperate with other external parties, including China and the EU. At the present time the prospects seem remote for achieving this obviously desirable objective. Yet the scale of tensions and potential humanitarian disasters arising from the absence of an effective strategic cooperation in this field seem certain to mount. Water flows into the dams of Kyrgyzstan and Tajikistan are declining, as are the virtual water reservoirs represented by the glaciers of the Pamir mountains. Water levels in the major reservoirs of both countries have fallen so substantially that there are increasing fears that these levels could descend to the 'dead level' (i.e. at which electricity generation becomes no longer possible).[30]

The conventional view of the IFIs is that progress over these vital projects is only conceivable if regional agreements could be reached between upstream and downstream states over the terms and conditions

---

[29] UNDP, "Central Asia Regional Risk Assessment", op. cit.
[30] Ibid.

for water discharge, with a strong foundation in international law. Yet the policy of the IFIs goes beyond the requirements of international law, which only calls for consultations with downstream states, not their mandatory agreement. A less stringent approach would call for the IFIs to go ahead with hydro investments in upstream Kyrgyzstan and Tajikistan on conditions that would take account of a reasonable interpretation of downstream interests. The EU, with its very large representation on the board of the World Bank, could be an important voice and vote in favour of such an approach.

However it would still be much preferable to advance on the basis of agreement between the upstream and downstream countries, given the serious risks of interstate conflict that could erupt. Given the difficulty the regional parties have in negotiating together, there is a case for a high-level diplomatic initiative, in which all major external parties (China, the EU, Russia, the US and the IFIs) would make a harmonised call for a cooperative solution, including the convening of a high-level conference to demonstrate the value of international agreements made in analogous situations elsewhere in the world.

Steps to facilitate this process include the 'Berlin Process' initiated by the German Foreign Minister in April 2008, with action under four headings: a) facilitation of cross-border water management, b) increase in the scientific expertise in cross-border water management, c) networking of water experts from the EU, Central Asia and Germany and d) creation of a degree programme in water management at the German Kazakh University in Almaty. The programme is being undertaken between 2009 and 2011 by GTZ with a budget of €10 million, in close cooperation with other regional and international partners. Action plans for regional institutional cooperation will aim at setting effective dispute settlement standards, the strengthening of cross-border river basin management through better dam coordination and the implementation of 'fast-track projects' such as the construction of smaller hydropower stations and irrigation plants.

Concrete proposals could also be advanced for consortium investments by both upstream and downstream countries in new hydro facilities, following a similar logic to that advanced above for the Ukraine gas transit pipeline.[31]

In the meantime the latest news in February 2009 is that Russia has gone ahead bilaterally with Kyrgyzstan with a pledge of a loan of $1.7 billion to invest in the Kambarata hydro project. This decision coincided with Kyrgyzstan's announcement that the US should leave the Manas airbase, which is currently serving as an important supply base for the war n Afghanistan. These developments have geo-political overtones, contrary to the hypothesis intended for the present report.

Conclusion: Since the collapse of the Soviet Union, cooperative management of the water, hydro-electric and irrigation resources of Central Asia has catastrophically broken down, resulting in growing humanitarian distress in upstream Kyrgyzstan and Tajikistan through a lack of winter heating, and in downstream Uzbekistan and Turkmenistan through water shortages for agriculture. The resulting internal and intra-state tensions are growing and could lead to open conflicts. The alert is being sounded by international agencies, but with little effect. The EU cannot itself become the main architect of a solution, but it could help shape a coalition of all major actors to this end, and in particular use its considerable weight in the board of the World Bank for a more pro-active approach.

---

[31] Such proposals have been made by Johannes Linn in "Need for Action on Central Asia Regional Water and Hydro-Energy Issues", Brookings Institution, Washington, D.C., 3 February 2009.

8. CLIMATE CHANGE

Search for a post-2012 climate change agreement

The EU is playing a leading role in the current negotiations to agree a successor to the Kyoto Protocol for action after 2012. The 2007 Bali Action Plan launched a two-year negotiation process with a clear deadline for the agreed outcome on cooperation beyond 2012 — the end of the first commitment period under the Kyoto Protocol — to be reached in Copenhagen in December 2009. The Action Plan calls for articulating "a shared vision for long-term cooperative action" and identifies four key elements that are likely to be part of a post-2012 framework: mitigation, adaptation, finance and technology. While the Poznan conference in 2008 was regarded as the halfway point, negotiations there did not result in a significant breakthrough. The EU has set its own target of greenhouse gas (GHG) emission reductions by 20% by 2020, which will be raised to 30% in the case of a wider international agreement; and called upon other developed countries, including the US, to follow their lead. In order to meet the EU objective of limiting the average global temperature rise to 2°C, the EU also suggested emissions reductions of 15-30% by 2020 by developing countries as a group, and especially what the Commission calls "economically advanced developing countries" or so-called 'emerging economies'. These commitments, binding for developed countries and non-binding for emerging economies, would make it possible to move towards a low-carbon economy in the coming decades.

Major polluters in the category of 'transition economies', which include Russia, Ukraine and Kazakhstan, may not have to adopt precisely the same obligations as developed countries, at least initially. The main concerns for these countries are: i) whether they would accept extending quantitative commitments for the next period when other emerging economies are strongly resisting to do so; ii) if so, what opportunities would arise from the continuation of existing tools such as Joint Implementation (JI) and trading of Assigned Amount Units (AAUs) or the introduction of innovative tools for the next period; and iii) how can transitional economies also benefit from increasing access to technology and finance which are to date mainly considered to be incentives for emerging economies to participate in the post-2012 framework.

The EU has already been helping Russia and Ukraine implement their compliance with the Kyoto Protocol. However this Kyoto phase has been almost a free ride for Russia and Ukraine, due to their reduction of CO_2 emissions with the collapse of Soviet-era industries in the early 1990s. For the next post-Kyoto period the EU could aim at cooperating in more ambitious plans for the three major carbon emitters – Russia, Ukraine and Kazakhstan. All three are major coal producers and users, and will need new state-of-the-art technologies for the cleaner burning of coal and carbon capture (as also Poland in the EU). Given the commonalities of these former Soviet states, there would be much to be said in favour of a cooperative endeavour between the EU, which has the best technologies available, and these three major polluters together. They share in addition similar problems of grossly inefficient energy use in both industry and households. The EU, and Germany in particular, has been making efforts in this direction.

The three major polluters

Russia. Until the global financial crisis Russia was benefiting from high oil prices and significantly increased its gross domestic product (GDP). As living standards improved, the consumption of electricity increased.[32] To meet increased demand, the old inefficient electricity generation capacity has been introduced again.[33] Moreover, the government has promoted a long-term strategy for the large-scale replacement of natural gas by coal in power generation in order to maximise the gas export.

Russia's greenhouse gas emissions have peaked at 1990 levels (approximately 3,300 million tonnes CO_2 equivalent, $MtCO_2$-eq),[34] for which the base year for the Kyoto Protocol target (stabilisation in 2008-12 at

---

[32] A. Kokorin and I. Gritsevich, "The danger of climate change for Russia: Expected losses and recommendations", Russian Analytical Digest, 23/07, DGO, Centre for East European Studies, Bremen, 2007.

[33] World Bank, "Energy Efficiency in Russia: Untapped Reserves", September 2008.

[34] For the Kyoto Protocol target, CO_2 emissions of the Russian Federation in 1990 were reported to be 2,388,720 giga-grams, which accounted for 17.4% of Annex I Parties' total CO_2 emissions in 1990.

1990 level) is set, experienced a fast decline in five years (1990-94) and a slow decline in the next five years (1994-98), and has recorded a gradual increase since 1999. In 2006 its GHG emissions are about 2,200 $MtCO_2$-eq.[35] This is the reason why Russia wants to keep the base year of 1990 for setting commitments for the post-2012 period. It regards a proposed 50% cut of global GHG emissions by 2050 as an 'aspirational goal', and stated its opposition to setting ranges for mid-term targets (25-40% cut by 2020 from 1990 levels) for it and other transition economies, noting that such mid-term targets should be based on national initiatives.

The Russian economy is characterised by a high share of energy-intensive sectors such as electric-power industry, metallurgy of ferrous and non-ferrous metals, oil refinery, chemicals and petro-chemicals. Their share accounts for more than 55% of total industrial production of the country.[36] Potential energy savings are estimated on the order of 360 to 430 million tonnes coal equivalent (Mtce) per year, broken down as follows: fuel and energy complex 120-135 Mtce; industry and construction 110-140 Mtce; transport 25-30 Mtce; agriculture 12-15 Mtce; residential buildings and appliances 95-110 Mtce.

The World Bank estimates that Russia can save 45% of its total primary energy consumption.[37] Achieving the full potential of Russia's energy efficiency would cost a total of $320 billion to the economy while saving about $80 billion per annum, which means paying back in only four years. Benefits to the total economy will amount to $120-150 billion per annum of energy cost savings.

Energy efficiency remains at centre of an ongoing bilateral dialogue on energy between the EU and Russia in order to secure Russia as a reliable supplier of oil and natural gas. These two parties have developed the EU-Russia Energy Dialogue since 2000, running three thematic groups, including one on energy strategies, forecasts and scenarios and another on

---

[35] http://unfccc.int

[36] EU-Russia Energy Dialogue, "Thematic Group on Energy Strategies, Forecasts and scenarios", Interim report, 2008.

[37] Op. cit., World Bank, 2008

energy efficiency.[38] Moreover, they launched the EU-Russia Energy Efficiency Initiative in 2006. Among others Russia appears to be interested in learning from the experience of the EU in addressing energy efficiency and energy savings in buildings, transport and electricity sectors.

In the 2003 Energy Strategy to 2020, Russia set a target of a 45% reduction in energy intensity by 2020. Currently the Ministry of Energy (Minenergo) is elaborating the draft of a new version of the Energy Strategy for Russia for the period up to 2030. The priorities of the Russian long-term energy policy would include a reduction of energy consumption by improvements in energy efficiency and a large-scale decrease in specific energy intensity on the order of 2.6 to 2.7 times by 2030, and securing a near-1990 level of GHG emissions in 2030. Then in 2008 the Ministry of Economic Development and Trade (MEDT) announced a new strategy, the "Concept of long-term socio-economic development" for the period up to 2020. In contrast to the Energy Strategy with its emphasis on the primary energy sources including oil, gas and coal, the development strategy calls for a shift to a more diversified economy, stressing the importance of high technology and innovation. Such a shift would contribute to GHG emissions reductions. As the Russian economy is particularly hit hard by the recent financial crisis and fall in oil prices, however, this economic forecast will have to be modified regarding GDP growth and energy consumption. Different ways of thinking across ministries described above would shadow the process of modifying scenarios under current economic circumstances.[39]

In June 2008 the President signed a Decree on measures to increase energy and eco-efficiency of the Russian economy. It aims at no less than a 40% cut in energy intensity per GDP unit by 2020 relative to 2007 and tasks

---

[38] Op. cit., EU-Russia Energy Dialogue, 2008. In parallel, the EU-Russia Environmental Dialogue is underway, covering a number of environmental issues such as climate change at the working group level.

[39] The 2020 Concept can be seen as a document of intentions to elevate Russia to a global leader in energy and innovation without articulating how to get there. Among others, Alexei Kudrin, the Minister of Finance, questioned how the ambitious strategy can be financed. See A.C. Kuchins et al., "Russia's 2020 Strategic Economic Goals and the role of international integration", IFRI and CSIS, July 2008.

the government to finish developing the action plan.[40] It is expected that regardless of changes to the long-term scenarios and strategies, energy efficiency will remain crucial for Russia's climate and energy policy in the short- to mid-term.

One of the main challenges posed in the Energy Strategy to 2020 is coal. Coal accounted for 26% of energy-related CO_2 emissions in Russia in 2005, one-half that of natural gas (52%).[41] The Energy Strategy projects a 75% increase in coal production and its increasing share in electricity generation in order to allow for more natural gas exports that are profitable. If an increasing use of coal is inevitable, the second best would be to promote the use of modern, efficient and cleaner technologies. To promote such technologies, especially the most efficient EU Clean Coal Technologies, the EU has viewed Russia as a priority under the CARNOT programme, attracting four projects underway. One of them is a study for Integrated Gasification Combined-Cycle (IGCC) technology possibilities in the Russian power sector, leading to CO_2 capture and hydrogen production.

In climate change Russia has formally entered the mode of complete observance of commitments under the Kyoto Protocol since June 2008. A comprehensive action plan has been adopted for compliance with the treaty. Russia can benefit from two instruments authorised under the Protocol, Joint Implementation (JI) and trading of Assigned Amount Units (AAUs).

Russia has achieved some progress in developing a legal framework for JI projects approval.[42] Nevertheless, Russia's JI project commission has not yet recommended the first project for approval.[43]

Another tool for Russia to realise its mitigation potential under the Kyoto Protocol is trading of AAUs, especially through a Green Investment

---

[40] S. Tulinov, "Presentation by the Russian Federation on mitigation potentials", by the Russian Federation at sixth session of the AWG-KP, Workshop on mitigation potentials, Poznan, 3 December 2008.

[41] Energy Information Administration, US.

[42] www.rusrec.ru

[43] On 29 January 2009, it was reported that the government was close to approving the first four JI projects (Pointcarbon, www.pointcarbon.com).

Scheme (GIS). The basic idea is to invest revenue from the sale of AAUs in projects that would lead to further emissions reductions. Russia's National Strategy in GHG emissions reductions (1998-99) links AAUs trading to green investments.[44] Despite an early expression of its own interest and support from the World Bank, Russia has been outpaced by other competitors with surplus AAUs, such as Hungary, Latvia, Ukraine and Romania in designing a GIS.[45]

Ukraine. Ukraine's GHG emissions also peaked at 1990 levels, the base year for the Kyoto Protocol target (stabilisation in 2008-12 at 1990 levels). It has recorded a steady decline in emissions until 2000 and since then a gradual increase. In 2006 its GHG emissions were reduced to less than a half of the base year levels. Hence Ukraine also argues for keeping the base year as 1990 for long-term GHG emissions reduction targets. However, in contrast to Russia, Ukraine is more open to target-setting at the UN negotiations, indicating the possibility for common targets for GHG emissions reductions by 20% by 2020 and 50% by 2050.[46]

The energy sector accounts for about 70% of Ukraine's total national GHG emissions. Between 1980 and 2004, its energy intensity was higher than that of Russia. Moreover, its heavy dependence on coal (40% of energy-related CO_2 emissions in 2004, next to natural gas 46%) makes the country high in carbon intensity. The government has introduced policies encouraging energy conservation and energy efficiency and passed a bill encouraging development of an alternative energy sector through tax

---

[44] A. Averchenkov, "Overall overview of the GIS instrument, its development and prospects for the Russian Federation", presentation at the Moscow Carbon Forum 2008, 28-29 April 2008.

[45] However, due to the economic downturn triggered by the financial crisis, it is estimated that there will be less demand for EU allowances (EUAs) needed for compliance with the EU emissions trading scheme, which is already reflected in a recent fall in the price of an EUA. Another factor is uncertainty about further commitments by developed and transition economies after 2012. Hence, seller countries with surplus AAUs may have been motivated to settle a deal rather quickly without searching for the best price.

[46] Ukraine, "Ideas and proposals on the elements contained in paragraph 1 of the Bali Action Plan", submissions from the parties to the UNFCCC AWGLCA, 27 August 2008.

rebates for companies seeking to develop solar, geothermal and wind power projects.[47]

Under the Kyoto Protocol Ukraine can benefit from both JI and AAU trading, ranked on top of the host country ratings. In its submission to the discussion on long-term cooperative action, the country suggests requiring Parties to fulfil commitments through 'greening' of carbon units.[48] Ukraine completed a World Bank study for a GIS in 2006 and has made progress in preparing for its introduction, including the adoption of procedures.[49] The country is also interested in a domestic emissions trading scheme, and participates as an observer in the International Carbon Action Partnership, an EU-led initiative for a platform linking domestic emissions trading schemes. The EU-Ukraine environmental dialogue has been upgraded and reactivated in 2006 from the bilateral working group on climate change initially launched in 2002.

Kazakhstan. While our information here is limited, Kazakhstan is ranked as the fourth most-GHG-intensive economy in the world. Coal accounts for 80% of the electricity production in the country.[50] It is reported that the President has signed a law on ratification of the Kyoto Protocol, thereby completing the ratification procedure. The country has pledged to take voluntary quantitative commitments for GHG emission reductions during the commitment period from 2008 to 2012 relative to 1992 levels. Ratification will make the country eligible for hosting projects under JI (Joint Implementation). Potential projects could be identified in the oil and gas, energy, metallurgical and cement sectors.

Scope for cooperation with the EU

A number of bilateral and multilateral initiatives have been already taking in place. The EU and Russia have developed dialogues on energy and environment respectively, and sought to increase synergy between the tracks. Some EU member states have been active in investing in JI projects

---

[47] Energy Information Administration, US.

[48] Ukraine, 2008, op. cit.

[49] O. Semkiv, "Recent GIS developments in Ukraine", presentation in Budapest, 25 April 2008.

[50] Energy Information Administration, US.

in order to purchase credits for their compliance with the Kyoto Protocol. The World Bank and the UNDP have helped potential host countries prepare for the legislation, institutions and procedures that are needed for approval of such projects. With so much untapped potential for energy efficiency and savings, Russia, Ukraine and Kazakhstan would prove to be a testing ground for the ability of existing and innovative mechanisms to attract private investments that are urgently needed to upgrade key sectors of the economy. Such tools would enable them to achieve further GHG emissions reductions and pursue paths to a low-carbon economy.

The EU could now propose a scheme to raise its climate change cooperation with Russia, Ukraine and Kazakhstan to a higher level with the following initiatives:

1) Invite Russia, Ukraine and Kazakhstan to join with the EU in a Quadripartite Climate Change Dialogue, given that the three post-Soviet states inherit many similarities in the climate change challenges they face, with potential economies of scale in solutions, and given also that this is a matter of common interest with a non-competitive logic (unlike so many other energy issues). This dialogue would provide leadership for identifying and getting political support for projects of common interest. In particular, the dialogue could contribute best practice in forecasting CO_2 emission trajectories and mitigation potentials, aid compliance over their (limited) commitments under the Kyoto Protocol and measures to ensure access to helpful instruments (JI and AAU).

2) Carbon Capture and Storage (CCS). The EU has now begun to work in Denmark and Germany on the first pilot projects for validating new technology for the capture of carbon dioxide (CO_2) from conventional power stations. A set of 10 such pilot projects are being supported by the EU. The EU could build on this experience by proposing to support CCS projects in third countries. For example there could be one CCS project in Russia, Ukraine and Kazakhstan, with major economies of scale, and benefits to be derived from preparing these cooperatively together.

3) Emissions Trading Schemes (ETS). Although the three countries are unlikely to enter into binding quantitative commitments at Copenhagen, this does not and should not prevent them from developing key national policy instruments aimed at GHG emissions reductions, of which ETS is a major item. The EU can help these

countries advance in the introduction of ETS schemes, and prepare for their linkage between each other and ultimately with the EU ETS.

4) Energy efficiency programmes. This very conventional heading covers many of the most basic requirements for energy savings, such as household metering and thermostatic controls and improvements on hugely wasteful old industrial technologies in all these countries. Energy efficiency measures could be a win-win solution, bringing benefits through GHG emissions reductions as well as improvements in local air quality. There have been many programmes and projects supported by the EU and member states (notably Germany), but their scale and impact seem still to fall short of what is urgently needed and technologically straightforward.

Conclusion: Three major countries – Russia, Ukraine and Kazakhstan – are all extremely heavy polluters, especially through the use of coal and obsolete energy-using technologies. They will resist inclusion in the group of developed countries making ambitious and binding quantitative commitments for the post-2012 period. However the EU could propose a collaborative action with all three countries together, setting up a Quadripartite Climate Change Dialogue, leading on to collaborative projects for Carbon Capture and Storage pilot projects, aiding the development of national emission trading schemes, and amplification of conventional energy efficiency and saving programmes.

9. BORDER MANAGEMENT

This section concerns border management and combating the trafficking of drugs, illegal migration and terrorism, which are of concern to the whole EU-Rus-EaP-CA area. For example drugs that mainly originate in Afghanistan transit through Central Asia and on into Europe through both southern routes through the Caucasus and Black Sea and northern routes through Russia. This is a relatively de-politicised subject, which should be open to increasingly deep cooperation between all parties.

The EU is already significantly engaged in border control assistance programmes and projects with all three partners (Rus, EaP and CA). This includes cooperation between Europol and Russian agencies. A primary objective is to get greater leverage in Central Asia. The EU already substantially funds the Border Management Programme for Central Asia (BOMCA), which is implemented by the UNDP. In addition there is activity of the United Nations Office on Drugs and Crime (UNODC), which is sponsoring projects to train Central Asian government agencies to curb drug traffic.

There are however serious challenges in organising effective cooperation between external assistance programmes and the host countries. In Central Asia, the Caucasus and Afghanistan, border authorities lack the experience and capacity needed to combat trafficking, illegal migration and terrorism across their borders. The strategic interests of the European Union are also at stake. Afghanistan's lagging border control efforts have enabled the Taliban to stage a comeback in remote frontier areas, and undermine US and EU efforts to help rebuild the shattered state.

Since the beginning of the 21st century, the European Union has made border management missions a part of its engagement with key regions. In the Caucasus, Central Asia and Afghanistan, the missions seek to enable states to perform basic elements of border management (see box below).

Basic elements of border management

- Staffing official crossings
- Policing unofficial crossings (green borders)
- Equipping border authorities
- Building border infrastructure
- Training and deploying customs officers, border police
- Defining the role of military units in border policing
- Drafting national border control policy
- Promoting cooperation across customs, police and the military
- Managing budgets of border control authorities
- Sharing information with foreign border control counterparts
- Harmonising border controls with neighbouring states
- Resolving incidents and preventing escalation

Border management missions can present three benefits. First, to prevent illegal and threatening flows of drugs (etc.) from approaching EU borders, and thus to reduce the cost of policing the EU's own external borders; second, to advance the European Union's foreign policy visibility and bolster its presence in key states; and third, to enable closer cooperation with Russia, which shares the same drug trafficking, illegal migration, weapons trade and cross-border terrorism problems as the EU.

The European Union should adopt a strategy to expand its border management missions while remaining mindful of complicating factors. Existing programmes reveal that it is difficult to teach states good border management. The process requires extended field presence, deep knowledge of the particular problems of host states, and efficient coordination with non-EU programmes. Future border management missions must build on the lessons learned by past initiatives. An additional complication is the lack of synergy between Commission programmes and national-level initiatives of EU member states. Many member states fund and sponsor bilateral border programmes abroad without coordination or deep consultation with the Commission.

EU-Russian Cross-Border Cooperation

In the sphere of border management, there have been two levels of cooperation with Russia. At the supra-national level, Brussels and Moscow have signed agreements and declared common interests in the fight against cross-border drug trafficking, illegal migration and drug terrorism. The most important ventures at this level are EUROPOL and FRONTEX. This cooperation is generally focused on the EU's external borders with Russia and tends to combat flows transiting from Russia. The benefit for the European Union could be important but Russia's willingness to cooperate seems half-hearted.

At the member-state level, cooperation over cross-border issues is more substantive, particularly for states that enjoy relatively better relations with Russia. German-Russian relations benefit from formal and informal cooperation in matters of cross-border trafficking and migration. Finland, which shares a long border with Russia, sponsored the Northern Borders Initiative. Such cooperation may be fruitful but lacks coordination or common purpose with EU-level programmes.

If cooperation along the Russian-EU border is limited, cooperation in matters of border management in Central Asia and the Caucasus is practically non-existent. One reason may be Moscow's frosty attitude to the EU's engagement in the Caucasus, Central Asia and Eastern Europe. Russia has tried to shut the European Union out of these regions in light of the latter's interests in promoting political reform, forging energy partnerships that decrease dependence on Moscow, and resolving local conflicts. Even before the Russian-Georgian war, Moscow was particularly irked at the European Union for sending a border support team to Georgia that included the borders of Abkhazia and South Ossetia in its mission. Russia has also displayed overt hostility to the OSCE, which was sometimes involved in training police and border authorities in Central Asia and the Caucasus.

Nonetheless, Russia has deeply compatible interests with the European Union when it comes to border management issues in Central Asia and the Caucasus, and border management missions provide a rare opportunity to recalibrate a specific aspect of EU policy to engage Russia. Until recently Russia was a key player in border control in Central Asia and the Caucasus. For example, upon becoming independent in 1991, some Central Asian states retained Russian military units to assist in border control. The last Russian border guards peacefully left Tajikistan and Kyrgyzstan in 2001, as the states deployed national border control forces. By re-involving Russia in regional border management assistance programmes, the European Union relieve strained ties and encourage Moscow to see the EU as a natural partner.

The EU's Role in Border Management Missions

The European Union has experience in funding and implementing border management missions in its periphery. It was critical in setting up functioning border services in Bosnia and Herzegovina. It is currently funding the EUBAM mission around Transnistria, which reinforces the capacity of Moldovan and Ukrainian officials to carry out effective border and customs controls and border surveillance. The EU and its member states also have a high profile in border management assistance in Central Asia and Afghanistan alongside the United States, NATO and the United Nations (see box below).

Border Management Assistance Sponsors in Eurasia and Afghanistan
- European Union, Commission (Policing and Border Missions)
- EU-member states (numerous initiatives)
- Organisation for Security and Cooperation in Europe (OSCE)
- United States (Department of Homeland Security, State Department, Department of Defense)
- North Atlantic Treaty Organization (NATO)
- United Nations Development Programme (UNDP)
- United Nations Office on Drugs and Crime (UNODC)
- Shanghai Cooperation Organisation (SCO)

The Border Management Programme for Central Asia (BOMCA) is funded by the European Union and implemented by the United Nations Development Programme. Inaugurated in 2000, BOMCA aims to export sound border control practices, enhance the border control capacity of participating states and teach officials to implement border policies that balance security with openness. BOMCA runs a multi-phase project that targets the technical and professional needs of Central Asian border authorities. BOMCA provides border authorities with basic equipment – from refrigerators to binoculars – and assists in the creation of border-crossing terminals. BOMCA also runs training programmes for border guards, encourages cross-border cooperation and promotes the adoption of integrated border management, which enables customs and border authorities to undertake operations jointly and more efficiently. BOMCA is in an advanced implementation phase, and its next goal is to assist Central Asian states to open high-volume trade corridors at select border crossings.

EU-funded BOMCA is an outstanding and innovative project, in that it is a region-wide programme with offices in all five Central Asian states. It employs a core staff of officers and managers who are EU citizens with direct experience in border management and development assistance. Each office also employs Central Asian nationals who are border control experts. This allows BOMCA to have intimate knowledge of each state's border control needs and enables it to liaise with Central Asian authorities. BOMCA has advanced its goals with a coordinated, region-wide strategy, and a multi-year budget of approximately €50 million.

In Afghanistan, the European Union works alongside the United Nations, NATO and the United States to raise the capacity of border control and customs. Afghanistan's serious border control deficiencies create alarming externalities in the broader Eurasian and Middle East regions. Most serious of these is the multi-billion euro cross-border transit of opiates and heroin that eventually make their way to the European Union.

The European Union's clearest involvement comes via the EUPOL and BOMBAF initiatives. Inaugurated in 2007, EUPOL Afghanistan aims to establish sustainable and effective civil policing arrangements to ensure appropriate interaction with the wider Afghan criminal justice system, including strategies for border management. The Border Management Programme for Badakhshan-Afghanistan (BOMBAF) is a European Commission-funded programme (UNDP implemented) focused on border management along the Afghan-Tajik border. Its budget (€5 million) supports a work plan that includes training border guards, provisioning border posts and encouraging community-based policing. Additionally EU member states participate in border management assistance bilaterally or through non-EU organisations. For example, Italian units under NATO command have provided extensive training of Afghan customs officers who will staff airports and border-crossing terminals. German police have also sponsored the training of Afghan border police. However, the programmes do not share information on progress and lessons learned and they do not report to the same agencies. Despite their direct and indirect EU ties, these initiatives lack common purpose and fail to pool their efforts.

Although there are many difficulties associated with border management assistance, recent political and strategic changes provide new opportunities for future border management missions. In Afghanistan, NATO plans to retrench its security and state-building efforts to core cities and roads. This will lead to greater demand for border management missions and the EU is particularly well-suited to rise to the task. In the process, the EU may also be able to engage Iran, which is currently fighting a low-intensity drug war along its border with Afghanistan and is quietly looking for international assistance to enhance its border controls. In Central Asia, Turkmenistan is undergoing a careful political opening and is more willing to work with foreign governments, particularly those that provide technical assistance. Tajikistan has shown unprecedented interest in drug interdiction but lacks resources to implement efficient border controls.

The Future of EU Border Management Missions

While the BOMCA project in Central Asia is a highly positive example, it currently suffers from two limitations. First, its EU identity is very reduced since it is operated by the UNDP and carries the various symbols of UNDP identity. Second, it has not sought to bring in Russian participation. The following proposals seek to remedy these limitations and more generally to build up a more effective border management programme in Central Asia. The model could be further extended with a twin regional project in the South Caucasus (a 'BOMSC').

An EU Regional Border Assistance Centre (RBAC): The EU would open this centre in a Central Asian capital city to serve as a coordinating hub for regional border management programmes, both EU and non-EU. The current programmes that directly and indirectly affect border management in Central Asia, the Caucasus and Afghanistan tend not to coordinate their activities or share information. The RBAC would promote coordination across border management missions, serve as a data repository and geographically map the missions and their activities. This would prevent duplication of effort and identify gaps in border assistance. Additionally, such a centre would serve as an early-warning detection mechanism for emerging security problems along borders and could propose response strategies.

The RBAC could be set up with a five-year mandate and a budget of €50 million. The centre would have a core EU staff including a director, political officers, border control experts, information technology experts and a smaller core of local staff to assist in liaising with national governments. Russia's participation would be encouraged, with reserved places for political officers and technical experts. The RBAC would enhance the profile of the EU by creating a visible on-the-ground presence. The creation of such a centre would be timely as the BOMCA draws down its mission in the coming years. The centre would brand border management as a holistic EU activity rather than one that member states take individually.

Many European Union member states deploy experts as Border Liaison Officers (BLOs) in border policing, customs enforcement and immigration policy. BLOs have played a useful role serving both as attachés at EU and member state diplomatic missions and in deployment to border 'hot spots'. However these resources need to work in closer coordination and on a large scale. The RBAC would further serve as a coordination bureau for these national experts and provide links to non-EU border programmes funded by the United States and the United Nations. A sum of about €15 million could enable the deployment of a few dozen additional BLOs for short-to-medium term stints over the next five years.

The RBAC could also oversee future EU border management initiatives in the Caucasus. Indeed, as EU-Russian tensions reduce, the Commission should consider replicating the BOMCA model with a twin regional project in the South Caucasus (a 'BOMSC').

An EU Fund for Border Management Reform (FBMR). The EU would take the lead in constituting a fund, to which member states and close partners of the EU such as Norway and Switzerland might also contribute, to encourage the states of Central Asia, Afghanistan and the Caucasus to apply competitively for funds for programmes to build up their border control capabilities. In Central Asia the RBAC would be the coordinating centre. The fund would require applicant states to diagnose their border control problems and propose solutions to them. Applications for technical or training assistance would then be vetted by a committee convened at the RBAC.

This fund should be designed to encourage Russia's involvement in border management. Russia could both contribute to the fund and appoint Russian border control experts alongside EU experts to vet applications and disburse funds. Russia would also be eligible to submit capacity-building projects for its southern borders.

The RBAC and its projects would also seek to establish working cooperation with the border-related activities in Central Asia of the Shanghai Cooperation Organization (SCO), in which China has strategic interests in relation to its frontier with Central Asia.

A five-year fund totalling €100 million could cover a range of small-to-large border control projects across Central Asia, Afghanistan and the Caucasus.

Conclusion: The EU and member states are already active in the field of border management in Eastern Europe and Central Asia. The challenges in Central Asia are especially daunting, being at the source of the drug trails from Afghanistan. The main EU efforts are in the UNDP-implemented BOMCA mission, which means lack of EU visibility and reduced strategic benefit. Proposals are made for the EU to establish regional border assistance centres in Central Asia and the Caucasus, with funds to amplify operations, and openings for Russia and third parties to join in.

10. CONFLICT RESOLUTION AND CIVIL EMERGENCIES

Separatist conflicts have been the most virulent source of tension in contemporary European affairs, with the post-conflict situation in Abkhazia and South Ossetia now to be arranged, and peace settlements to be sought still for Transnistria and Nagorno Karabakh, and a conflict prevention action needed in Crimea. In all these cases there could be benefits to be achieved if Russia were willing to work in a sincerely cooperative spirit with the EU and the other post-Soviet states concerned.

Transnistria has seen two model solutions. The Russian 'Kozak memorandum' of 2004 was a federative proposition with some quite standard constitutional features. But fatally it so overloaded the weight of Transnistrian representation that President Voronin refused to sign. Since 2006 there has been a Voronin 'package deal' on the table (at least not in published form), whose main components are autonomy for Transnistria, confirmed neutrality, withdrawal of foreign troops and assured property rights in Transnistria (i.e. no re-privatisation). The negotiation format is most active at the level of bilaterals between Chisinau, Tiraspol and Moscow, with less activity so far in the 5+2 format (Russia, Ukraine, OSCE, EU, US + Moldova and Transnistria). Russia could rehabilitate its reputation considerably with a willingness to back a reasonable compromise. The EU should push forcefully for the 5+2 format to be the principal negotiating forum. It should do this with the aid of a high-level political representative for Moldova, with the professional support of the existing special representative, for example Aleksander Kwasniewski, former President of Poland.

The post-war situation of Abkhazia and South Ossetia is the subject of the Geneva talks on security arrangements and IDP (internally displaced persons) return issues, which began on 15 October 2008, with the participation of Russia, Georgia, EU, US, OSCE and UN. The non-recognition of the independence of these two entities by any party except Russia has presented difficulties from the start. One scenario, in due course, could see functional cooperation with both Abkhazia and South Ossetia by all parties, including the EU, but without formal recognition of these new de facto states. There will be political reluctance to grant even this degree of implicit partial recognition, given that it may be perceived as a concession to Russia, which provoked the war. On the other hand, Abkhazia (more than South Ossetia) does not want to become part of the Russian Federation, but rather wants to start to develop now as part of modern Europe. This objective should be met with an open EU position for economic relations and people contacts. A move by the EU to cooperate functionally with Abkhazia and South Ossetia without recognition could be reciprocated by Russia over Kosovo, with it moving to a position of abstention, rather than seeking constantly in UNSC meetings to block EU actions there.

For Nagorno Karabakh there has been years of attempts by the OSCE-sponsored Minsk Group co-chairs (France, Russia, US) to mediate a settlement in Nagorno Karabakh, and several episodes where agreement seemed close at hand. The content of these proposed settlements has been kept secret, but elements seem to include cession by Armenia of the occupied territories surrounding NK, guaranteed transport corridors for both NK into Armenia and for Nakichevan into Azerbaijan-proper, and deferral of a final status agreement for NK. Ideas for settlement of the constitutional regime have included a special status for NK with links to both Armenia and Azerbaijan, which would be consistent with the province's history over the centuries at the interface between Ottoman, Russian and Persian empires. NK could be open to the economies of both Armenia and Azerbaijan, with a provision for refugee return, notably to the former Azeri-majority town of Sushi.

Russia and Turkey both now seek to take the initiative over NK unilaterally. President Medvedev hosted a meeting in Moscow in late 2008 with both Armenian and Azeri leaders. Turkey for its part seems to be moving towards normalisation of its relations with Armenia, with a view to mediating also with Baku over Nagorno Karabakh. The process might start with an opening of the Turkish-Armenian frontier for normal trade and movement of people, the removal of remaining Armenian claims (e.g. implicit in its constitution) to its earlier territorial frontiers, and moves in favour of historic reconciliation. In a further step Turkey might try its hand at mediating a settlement of the Nagorno Karabakh conflict. The EU could join with Turkey and Russia in taking a lead to get a settlement. Another formula might see a reconfiguration of the Minsk Group to include Turkey with France's role converted into an EU role.

Finally on Crimea, whose destabilisation must be avoided. Russia's intentions are suspect on account of numerous semi-official/unofficial speeches and activities by Russian nationalist elements, including mayor Luzhkov of Moscow, notably contesting the commitments under the Sebastopol Treaty of 1997 to withdraw the Russian Black Sea Fleet by 2017, and stirring up inter-ethnic tensions with the Tartar communities. Official Russian spokesmen confirm plans to evacuate Black Sea fleet to Novorossisk, and indication of progress in building the new base and a date for the move to begin would be a strong confidence-building measure. It would be further helpful for the Russian authorities to use their influence to cool down Russian nationalist activism that aggravates tensions in Crimea, and for the EU to urge Kiev to employ exemplary policies towards the non-Ukrainian nationalities (Russian and Tartar) in Crimea. These national minority issues could be subject to conflict prevention initiatives, which are relevant to the responsibilities of the OSCE High Commissioner for National Minorities. In addition there could be of initiatives of civil society organisations, to which the EU and/or member states might contribute, with European experts also usefully contributing as a neutral party between the Ukrainian and Russian interests.

Civil emergencies

Both the EU and Russia have invested in considerable capacities for emergency aid in the case of natural disasters bringing humanitarian distress. This is a non-controversial field in which there could be established a coordination framework bringing in also the Eastern partner states and Central Asia. Such a Pan-European Civil Emergencies Facility would develop operational procedures for common actions, and coordinate supply capabilities and logistics.

Conclusion: The conflict resolution and prevention agenda in East European states is an obvious candidate in theory for EU-Russian collaboration, together with the interested third states directly concerned (in the South Caucasus, and cases of Transnistria and Crimea). Russia has however taken the view that the perpetuation of these conflicts was in its tactical geo-political interests, until and unless circumstances such as the August war with Georgia presented the opportunity for decisive 'victory'. However this policy has contributed heavily to Russia's poor reputation in European affairs. In the hypothesis of this paper Russia might be induced to change this stance, and join with the EU in genuine conflict resolution and prevention efforts, in which case there could be a remarkable turn around in favour of cooperative outcomes. A Pan-European Civil Emergencies Facility is also proposed.

11. Networks of Civil Society and Political Development

Network of Schools of Political Studies

The 'Schools of Political Studies', sponsored by the Council of Europe with the financial support of the European Commission, aim to train the next generation of political, economic, social and cultural leaders in the countries in transition. The schools organise seminars and conferences on such themes as European integration, democracy, human rights, the rule of law and globalisation in which national and international experts take part.

The first School of Political Studies was founded in Moscow in 1992, as a private initiative resolved to help the creation of a new Russian democratic political elite. The Moscow model proved so impressive that it was copied in many European transition countries, mainly those that were not candidates for accession to the EU. There are currently schools in Russia, Ukraine, Moldova, Georgia, Armenia, Azerbaijan and most south-east European countries. A project to create a school in Belarus is under development. While the Moscow school was the pioneer, its operations have been made increasingly difficult during the years of the Putin presidency and the restrictive and intrusive NGO law introduced there a few years ago. The school has survived so far, still directed by Elena Nemirovskaya, and participates fully in the now substantial network. However its recent proposal of a major project to extend its activities in the regions of Russia was refused funding by the European Commission on grounds of insufficient budgetary resources.

Each school is run by a director, appointed by a board to select candidates (about 40 per year), prepare study programmes and deal with the school's financial and administrative management. The schools of political studies are national NGOs in their own countries. They operate in regional networks and organise regional activities, particularly in the Balkans and the Caucasus. The schools' directors meet several times a year to coordinate their activities and exchange experience and good practice.

Alumni associations have been set up by a majority of the schools, helping to maintain and develop professional and social ties. Among the schools' alumni are many ministers, members of Parliament, local councillors, senior officials, magistrates, businessmen, journalists, etc. The schools' study programme is run by the Directorate General of Democracy and Political Affairs of the Council of Europe, which encourages synergy between the schools and the Council of Europe's activities in the countries involved in the programme.

Since their foundation, each of the schools of political studies has participated in its annual Summer University in Strasbourg, focusing mainly on the European institutions. This major event brings together all participants of the schools of political studies (numbering around 600), with debate and reflection on common issues, and spaces created for bilateral and regional dialogue. Each year's Summer University is dedicated to a particular topic, with plenary sessions gathering all of the participants, and thematic conferences grouping from 2 to 4 schools of political studies. Visits to the European Court of Human Rights are organised.

In an effort to further enhance the visibility, growth and consolidation of the schools of political studies, the Council of Europe announced in 2008 the establishment of the European Association of the Schools of Political Studies. The Association will have no profit-making, political or religious purpose. It will be administered by a board of administration consisting of Council of Europe officials and the directors of several schools of political studies, to be elected for four years by the general assembly of members.

The schools of political studies are a joint programme between the Council of Europe and the European Commission, which currently share 50/50 the budget, with the Commission contributing currently €1.7 million for two years, with additional financial contribution made by member states. To exploit fully the potential of this family of schools there should be a larger sustained budget on the order of €4-5 million.

Network of public policy think tanks (PASOS)

The PASOS network was founded in 2004 at the initiative of the Open Society Institute (OSI) as an association of independent think tanks in Central and Eastern Europe and Central Asia. Its headquarters are in Prague. It currently has 31 member institutes (see box below). PASOS members provide policy advice to the region's decision-makers and international organisations on issues such as democracy, rule of law, good governance, respect for and protection of human rights and economic and social development It has received support from the EU, UNDP, the UK (DFID), OSI and various other international foundations and national governments. PASOS has the classic goals of think tanks: to assist public policy-making through conferences, seminars, workshops and publications, to foster cooperation between network members, and to support research and analytical capacity of high quality.

PASOS member organisations

Russia

Strategia - St. Petersburg Center for Humanities and Political Studies, St Petersburg, Russian Federation

Eastern Europe

Social Policy and Development Center (SPDC), Yerevan, **Armenia**

Economic Research Center (ERC), Baku, **Azerbaijan**

Center for Economic and Social Development (CESD), Baku, **Azerbaijan**

Institute for Policy Studies (IPS), Tbilisi, **Georgia**

Caucasus Institute for Peace, Democracy and Development (CIPDD), Tbilisi, **Georgia**

Institute for Public Policy (IPP), Chisinau, **Moldova**

Institute for Development and Social Initiatives (IDIS "Viitorul"), Chisinau, Moldova

Expert-Group, Chisinau, **Moldova**

International Centre for Policy Studies (ICPS), Kyiv, **Ukraine**

Central Asia

Public Policy Research Center (PPRC), Almaty, **Kazakhstan**

Center for Public Policy (CPP), Bishkek, **Kyrgyzstan**

PASOS also has member organisations in Albania, Bulgaria, Croatia, Czech Republic, Estonia, Hungary, Kosovo, Latvia, Macedonia, Poland, Romania, Slovakia, Slovenia, and Serbia.

The enlargement of the EU has brought new dimensions to this task. The EU has moved to the borders of Ukraine, Belarus, Russia and Moldova. On the one hand this has resulted in a more marked division of transition countries in the former Soviet bloc between EU members and those with prospects for membership, and those who are excluded. On the other hand the think tanks of the new EU member states have both skills and motivation to work with their counterparts in Eastern Europe and Central Asia.

The evident challenge is to build up this network with a critical mass of institutes and individuals of outstanding quality. This requires long-term investments in the education and professional development of scholars, policy analysts and communicators with first-class professional skills, and their linkage in a network of institutes which should include leading think tanks of the EU, especially in the new member states.

The PASOS experience is so far only a beginning, since its funding is on a small scale, and it is heavily dependent on the Open Society Institute. The challenge now is to find the resources and leadership to develop the network more strongly, and to diversify the funding. Several US-based private international foundations have made exemplary contributions in this field. Apart from the OSI network there is the example of the Carnegie Endowment for International Peace, which has been able to sustain a first-class think tank centre in Moscow, despite the Putin regime's serious harassment of such activities.

The EU, its member states (e.g. the German political foundations), and various European private foundations (e.g. VW Stiftung, Compagnia di San Paolo, Swedish Jubileum fund) are active in this field, but without critical mass as of yet. These three European foundations have however begun to operate as a consortium in research activities on EU foreign and security policy, and support think tank activity also in the Balkans. The way ahead might be for the European Commission and a few seriously interested member states to propose to these foundations a collaborative project. Experience shows that this kind of politically sensitive activity should be led by independent private foundations, but the needed critical mass of funding requires also official support. For example a central coordinating institute should have a budget of around €3 million, and a network of a dozen institutes might receive core grants of about €1 million each, thus totalling around €15 million per annum.

Network of Institutes and Schools of Public Administration (NISPAcee)

The Network of Institutes and Schools of Public Administration in Central and Eastern Europe (NISPAcee) was established in 1994 in response to the needs that came to light with the immense political, economic, and social transformation in the Central and Eastern European region. These needs were interconnected to the role of the state and public administration throughout CEE and the former Soviet Union in the transition to a market economy, liberal, multi-party democracy and the rule of law.

NISPAcee, with headquarters in Bratislava, is a nongovernmental, non-profit, professional membership organisation, whose members are educational, training and research institutions in the area of public administration and public policy from all formerly communist countries. At present more than 120 institutions from the region are NISPAcee members and almost 40 associate members from the EU and the US. The NISPAcee members represent the most important and influential institutions in the region, of which a selection is listed in the box below. In addition NISPAcee maintains a larger database of more than 1000 relevant institutions and 4000 individuals from the region.

Network of Institutes and Schools of Public Administration in Central and Eastern Europe (NISPAcee)

Russia: Northwestern Academy of Public Service, St. Petersburg

Russian Academy of Public Administration, Moscow

Siberian Academy of Public Administration, Novosibirsk (and 11 other institutes)

Ukraine: Lviv Regional Institute of Public Administration, NAPA

National Academy of Public Administration, Office of the President of Ukraine, Kyiv

Odessa Regional Institute of Public Administration, NAPA (and 4 other institutes)

Belarus: Academy of Public Administration under the aegis of the President of the Republic of Belarus, Minsk

Moldova: Academy of Public Administration, Chisinau

Caucasus Countries

Georgia: Georgian Institute of Public Affairs (and 3 other institutes)

Armenia: Public Administration Academy of the Republic of Armenia (and 2 other institutes)

Azerbaijan: Academy of Public Administration under President of Azerbaijan (and 1 other)

Central Asia

Kyrgyzstan: Academy of Management under the President of Kyrgyz Republic

Kazakhstan: The Academy of Public Administration under the President of the Republic of Kazakhstan

Tajikistan: Institute of Training of Civil Servants

New Member States of the EU

Bulgaria: Institute of Public Administration & European Integration (and 9 other institutes)

Czech Republic: Institute of State Administration, Ministry of the Interior of the Czech Republic (and 6 other institutes)

Estonia: Estonian Public Service Academy (and 3 other institutes)

Hungary: Faculty of Public Administration, Corvinus University of Budapest (and 9 other institutes)

Latvia: Latvian School of Public Administration (and 3 other institutes)

Lithuania: Lithuanian Institute of Public Administration (and 8 other institutes)

Romania: National Institute of Administration (and 11 other institutes)

Slovakia: Institute of Public Administration, Ministry of Interior (and 6 other institutes)

Slovenia: Administration Academy, Ministry of Public Administration of Slovenia (and 3 other institutes)

Founders of NISPAcee stressed that countries in transition had common problems and international cooperation of academicians and practitioners could have a critical contribution to coping with these problems and shorten the time of transition. NISPAcee had emerged as a regional facility for the exchange of knowledge, experience and skills and as a cohesive force of efforts to cope with challenges in the field of public administration and it has become an essential facilitator in regional progress. The new EU member states have special capabilities to assist the less advanced transition countries, which NISPAcee can mobilise. NISPAcee is an integral part and an active partner in the increasing and intensive flow of ideas and human contacts between what is Europe by historical tradition and the new geopolitically defined larger Europe and Central Asia. Public administration has to increase and strengthen the use of market-type mechanisms.

An increasing diversity has emerged in the NISPAcee region in the progress of transition, with very different levels and paces of transition. Partly this is related to the differences in starting conditions in levels of development, but also varying readiness to overcome transition problems. It is also partly related to the changes in the eastern borderline of Europe. The task is to strengthen cooperation between the scholars and practitioners of the various countries, to create a common ground for cooperation and to provide a forum that might be interesting for and could serve the interest of all professionals engaged with problems of their own country and sub-regions.

There is a need to upgrade core governmental capacities in all targeted countries to strengthen strategic thinking in government for making critical future-shaping choices and for understanding of advantages of wide-ranging cooperation at least in economic, political and security spheres. Several parallel streams of actions could be taken in order to achieve this core goal, namely: to prepare and utilise forward-looking studies as a policy compass; to build qualified strategy-oriented units at the central level of government; to develop specific programmes and courses at universities and in-service institutes to provide advanced professional training in strategic issues, public policy and administration; to upgrade citizenship preparation at high school and universities; to encourage public discussions and consultations among politicians, mass media commentators, academics and intellectuals, grass root activists, etc. on main national policy issues.

The European Commission launched a project on an establishment of the Regional School of Public Administration – ReSPA for the Western Balkans in 2004, leading in January 2009 to its permanent location in Montenegro. NISPAcee could provide the basis for a similar institution for Eastern neighbour states, Russia and Central Asia.

A full development of this programme would require a budget of about €5 million, compared to the current operations of NISPAcee costing €1 million.

Conclusion: This set of three networks in the broad civil society and public policy field illustrates how it is possible to organise politically sensitive activity overarching the former Soviet bloc, from Eastern Europe to Central Asia. These networks are plausible candidates for stronger support by the EU, member states and European private international foundations. The sums suggested, totalling €25 million, for all three networks would mean a substantial increase on present funding, but these are not large sums in relation to total ENPI resources.

12. PAN-EUROPEAN SECURITY ORDER

President Medvedev has been promoting the idea of a pan-European security treaty, including in speeches made in Berlin on 5 June 2008 and again in more detail in Evian on 8 October. One could readily agree that the August 2008 war in Georgia signalled the breakdown of the European security order, and the need to avert any further such developments. Moreover the unresolved Transnistria and Nagorno Karabakh conflicts and simmering tensions in Crimea are all cases that are vulnerable to escalating tensions and possible violence.

First, however, it is opportune to recall the content of the existing pan-European security treaty, the Helsinki Final Act of August 1975, negotiated with the Soviet Union, of which the OSCE is custodian. Since the end of the Soviet Union the OSCE (formerly CSCE) has seen its membership enlarge to include all former Soviet republics, including Central Asia. It is therefore constituted in line with the objectives of the present study. But the OSCE now functions at a low level of achievement. Should its founding principles be revisited? One might think so after over 30 years. Is it obsolete?

The Act's "Declaration on Principles Guiding Relations between Participating States" enumerated the following 10 points:

I.   Sovereign equality, respect for the rights inherent in sovereignty
II.   Refraining from the threat or use of force
III.   Inviolability of frontiers
IV.   Territorial integrity of States
V.   Peaceful settlement of disputes
VI.   Non-intervention in internal affairs
VII.   Respect for human rights and fundamental freedoms
VIII.   Equal rights and self-determination of peoples
IX.   Co-operation among States
X.   Fulfilment in good faith of obligations under international law

As a set of norms for international security relations, these old texts remain absolutely valid; not a word is out of date. What then does President Medvedev propose? His speeches contain no references to OSCE, although Russia participates now in diplomatic discussions on this topic in OSCE fora. Medvedev identified Russia's priorities under five points in his Evian speech:

1. *Political norms: respect for international law, sovereignty, territorial integrity, political independence of states.* These largely conform with the Helsinki Final Act. However principle VII from Helsinki on human rights is omitted, while in the August war with Georgia Russia breached Helsinki principles III and IV.

2. *Security norms: inadmissibility of use of force or threat of its use in international affairs, and a unified approach to conflict settlement and peacekeeping.* This is also following the Helsinki Final Act, but in the war with Georgia, Russia was in breach of principle II restraining the use of force.

3. *The guarantee of equal security and three 'no's', namely:*
   - *No ensuring one's own security at the expense of others.* This is unclear. How can one define whether a measure for one's own security is at the expense of others? Is a defensive alliance at the expense of the security of another neighbour? The target of the language seems to be the US missile defence project.
   - *No allowing acts (by military alliances or coalitions) that undermine the unity of the common security space.* This implies that the common space exists, which is hardly the case; or maybe it is referring to a common space that should be created, in which case its mechanisms need to be explicit.
   - *No development of military alliances that would threaten the security of other parties to the Treaty.* This presumably targets NATO expansion, and maybe that of the EU if it became more of a military alliance.

4. *No state or international organisation can have exclusive rights to maintaining peace and stability in Europe.* This seems to be just a rhetorical statement, expressing resentment towards the US, NATO or the EU.

5. *Establish basic arms control parameters and reasonable limits on military construction. Also needed are new cooperation procedures and mechanisms in areas such as WMD proliferation, terrorism and drug trafficking.* This

heterogeneous rubrique seems first to be proposing a renegotiation of the Conventional Forces in Europe (CFE) Treaty, and goes on to propose a new or improved non-proliferation regime. Cooperation over terrorism is already on the agenda of G8, OSCE and EU-Russia relations. Cooperation over drug trafficking is plausible, for example together with the UN Office on Drugs and Crime (UNODC) in Central Asia in particular.

To summarise, the Medvedev proposal assembles a menu of items which start with some norms extracted from the Helsinki Final Act of 1975, several of which were breached by Russia in the August war with Georgia, followed by some newly formulated pseudo-norms that obviously seek to stop NATO's expansion, and ends with a set of conventional security topics that are already on the agenda of international organisations and bilateral EU or US-Russia relations.

We will return to the NATO question in a moment, but we first look at reasons why the OSCE has not flourished and is not even mentioned by Medvedev. Within the OSCE itself there has been a debate in the last few years over its priorities, with Russia wanting to downplay work on democracy and election monitoring. But if it has to be like that within the OSCE, the result will be that the EU will do more on its own, for which it has the resources and experience. But this reallocation of tasks will only further weaken the only truly pan-European security organisation.

Responses to the Medvedev proposals at OSCE meetings have been mixed, ranging from the Sarkozy proposal to hold a special OSCE Summit on the subject (which has not been agreed), to remarks that the existing security architecture should be used better (e.g. in Russia's observance of OSCE principles and decisions), through to the ambiguous position of the new US administration.[51] The EU seems not to have made any substantive statement on the subject, but many European countries at the last OSCE ministerial in December 2008 seemed to have stressed the need for a comprehensive view of security. It is nonetheless positive that diplomatic

---

[51] At the EU-US summit meeting in Prague on 5 April 2009, President Obama called for eliminating the threat of nuclear war throughout the world and committed the United States to reducing its nuclear arsenal, yet said that the US missile defence system in the Czech Republic and Poland "will go ahead as long as the threat from Iran exists".

dialogue is now underway within OSCE on the Medvedev proposals, and for these to take place within the OSCE is in itself a confidence-improving step.

To be fair to Russia, the EU is itself responsible for a large part of the OSCE's political obsolescence and unwieldy procedures. OSCE has now 56 member states, all in principle enjoying the same sovereign equality, from Andorra and the Vatican to Russia and the United States, but with the EU only present as an observer. Its meetings resemble a mini-UN General Assembly. The EU accounts for almost half of the seats around a very large table, to which may be added the tendency nowadays for most of non-EU Europe to align on the EU's foreign and security policy declarations, with the result that the EU27 often becomes a 42-country bloc. The EU member states account for 70% of the OSCE's budget. Is it not time now for the EU to contribute a serious rationalisation of its presence in the OSCE, given the advances of its foreign and security policies, and the needs that are now obvious in view of Europe's dysfunctional security order?

A first step would be for the EU to become a full member of OSCE, which together with the Lisbon Treaty innovations in the CFSP area, would be a catalyst for the EU member states to do better in arriving at common positions. Given the cumbersome workings of the OSCE at the level of all 56 member states, a further step would be to test recourse to restricted core group meetings, for example on a tripartite basis (EU-RUS-US), or on a wider basis including other major countries such as Turkey and Ukraine. There have been some examples of this practice already in OSCE, but without being institutionalised.

At a later stage, as and when there would have been some successful confidence-building episodes, there might be consideration of a more ambitious and structured reform measure, creating a 'European Security Council', following in some respects the model of the UN Security Council. A permanent European Security Council could consist of major states including for example Turkey and Ukraine beyond G8 members with the EU, with further rotating places such as one for the rest of non-EU Europe and one for Central Asia. Russia has in the past made proposals for something like a European Security Council, but these were interpreted, probably correctly, as seeking to acquire a veto power over European security matters, and were therefore never pursued. However the political role of such a body does not have to be formulated in such an obviously unacceptable form.

We return now to Russia's major demand for the European security architecture, that NATO should not press on with further enlargement into the post-Soviet space. A narrative deeply ingrained in the Russian political consciousness is that Gorbachev and Yeltsin were duped by the West over NATO enlargement, and that Kohl had given Gorbachev assurances that NATO would not be expanded to Russia's frontiers in exchange for Gorbachev's cooperation over German re-unification. Those supporting NATO's further enlargement to include Ukraine and Georgia argue that any independent sovereign state in Europe has the right to apply for NATO membership, and no third party has the right to tell them otherwise. That is a serious argument, but it not the whole story. NATO membership involves the solemn commitment under Article 5 to take an attack on any member's territory as an attack on all. The counterpart to this strategic commitment is that the aspiring member state has to be a reliable partner. It has to be solidly behind the alliance politically, with no doubts over the credibility of its own commitment. It has also to have demonstrated sustained reliability for sound political judgment on strategic matters in times of stress. These two criteria – national consensus and political reliability – might well be adopted more explicitly by NATO, rather like the EU adopted its Copenhagen criteria for its enlargement.

Neither public opinion nor the political parties in Ukraine are anywhere near united on the NATO question. The criterion should be far more than majority parliamentary support, and essentially a national consensus. And Georgia, while united behind the wish to be protected by NATO, has demonstrated precisely the reverse of sober reliability in matters of strategic behaviour.

These weaknesses were evident enough already before the Bucharest summit, which attached no timetable to its forecast that Georgia and Ukraine "will be" members of NATO, some day. The candidates' lack of qualifications for NATO membership has become even more evident since then. NATO will surely not reverse its Bucharest declaration, but it could move to define its 'Copenhagen criteria'.

It would surely be best if some significant confidence-building measures could be set in motion alongside the general discussion of the Medvedev proposals. An example could be a genuinely cooperative move towards resolution of the Transnistria conflict, for which a 5+2 body (which includes the EU) has been set up in principle, but whose activation is being held up by Russia. There may be other less demanding steps that could be much easier to initiate but still useful, as suggested by the recent start of tri-lateral (German-Polish-Russian) consultations between foreign policy planning staffs, whose positive political symbolism is striking.

In due course, as and when some confidence between Russia's leadership and the West is restored, there could be a return to explore possibilities for improving the Russia-NATO relationship. It is a striking anomaly that during the eight years of the Putin presidency there were only two meetings at the summit level between NATO and Russia. The problem is again at least in part on the European side, whose numerous small states make for the unwieldy 26+1 format (becoming now 28+1 with the addition of Albania and Croatia and more to come) for NATO-Russia relations. To counter this one could innovate with a new G4 summit format for pan-European security affairs, bringing together Russia, the US, NATO represented by its secretary general, and the EU represented by its post-Lisbon presidency and high representative. This G4 could be considered as an alternative or complement to the hypothesised OSCE European Security Council.

Returning back to immediate practicalities, one may ask whether early results could flow in the event of a better personal chemistry between the next US President and the Russian leadership. Is it too late for the missile defence project to be made into a matter for operational cooperation, given that it is meant to address a common hypothetical threat from a rogue nuclear state, with Iran in mind in particular? A precise Russian argument is that the radar facilities to be installed in the Czech Republic could be used to track missiles launched from Russia, and so would alter the strategic balance of nuclear strike capabilities, and upset the (nuclear-strategic) logic of mutually assured destruction (M.A.D.). Is this so? If not, transparent consultations in good faith should dispel the concern. If it is so, then there is an issue for a next round of START talks. There is also the broader question of arms control, including for conventional weapons, raised in the Medvedev proposals. Initiation of procedures for negotiations could become a valuable confidence-building measure.

Conclusion: Russia has proposed a new pan-European security architecture, which sounds promising at first sight, even if the credibility of Russia's intentions have been undermined in the war with Georgia and its recognition of Abkhazia and South Ossetia. While many of the details of President Medvedev's proposals are unlikely to win widespread support, both the EU and NATO reflect on how to respond, and possibly to give this initiative a positive turn. For example the EU might respond by taking two steps to reinforce OSCE, whose role remains entirely pertinent: first, for the EU to become a full member of OSCE, and second, more ambitiously at a later stage as and when confidence between the parties had been seriously improved, to propose consideration of a new European Security Council which would be for a core group of major players within OSCE.

13. OTHER PAN-EUROPEAN MULTILATERALISM

The existing pan-European regional-multilateral institutional infrastructure is quite significant, and should in principle play a significant part in any broad plan to enhance cooperation across this continental space. However politico-institutional limitations are often severe, as the following examples (in addition to that of the OSCE already discussed above) show.

The Council of Europe should in principle play a valuable role in achieving convergence on European standards of democracy. It has been hindered in recent years by Russia's 'exceptionalism', in objecting to political criticisms from the rest of Europe, and aggressively advocating its own (dubious) conception of 'sovereign democracy'. However the EU has been increasing its cooperation with the Council of Europe, with funding of relatively low-profile but professional projects in the democracy/rule-of-law/civil-society domains, bringing together all member states including Russia. It is notable that low-profile but professional projects in these domains are appreciated by Russian participants, marking a dichotomy between the aggressively assertive and divergent top-level political discourse, and willingness at the professional level to join in cooperative programmes. It is also positive that Russia has largely respected the judgements of the European Court of Human Rights, including a considerable number of highly sensitive cases involving plaintiffs from Chechnya where the court rules against the Russia government.

Given Kazakhstan's interest in developing its European connections, consideration could be given to devising a special cooperation agreement and programme between the Council of Europe and Kazakhstan.

In the economic domain the EBRD has become a well established and respected institution. Its role has been changing as the EU's new member states graduated out of the transition category, while its emphasis on operations in Rus-EaP-CA has correspondingly become more important. It is notable that the EBRD has found an important niche activity with which

Russia is comfortable and fully supportive. Russia sees the EBRD as an interesting partner not only for investment in Russia, but also for partnership with some of its own major investors in Eastern Europe. The logic here is that Russian investors are not really trusted to be free of political control, or for their methods of corporate governance, but these problems – actual or just perceived – could be eased if the EBRD took significant minority shareholdings in Russian investments in countries such as Poland or Ukraine. The case of the proposed Ukraine gas transit pipeline (as discussed above in section 6) could be a flagship example of such partnerships.

The Energy Charter Treaty (ECT) was intended to serve exactly the purposes of cooperation between EU-Rus-EaP-CA. The Treaty has got stuck over Russia's non-ratification, and especially its refusal to agree the draft transit protocol, which would oblige pipeline operators to grant access to third-party suppliers of gas (e.g. for Turkmenistan gas to pass freely on normal commercial terms through Russian pipelines, thus undermining Gazprom's monopolistic control power). In reaction to the January 2009 Ukrainian gas transit crisis, the Russian side declared that "the Energy Charter proved to be useless, despite Ukraine's ratification of it", to which the Ukrainian side replied that it was Russia that cut off supplies. The Russian side argues that it would like to see a more adequate legal order for energy transit in Europe, but is dismissive of the ECT. The Secretary-General of the ECT could only lament the failure by Russia and Ukraine to respect the principle of regular supplies, or to use dispute settlement procedures that the ECT already provides (see his statement in the box below).

The question now posed is whether the Energy Charter Treaty, which has not been able to function to its full potential, could be modernised to bring it into the operational mainstream with the aid of some revisions and additional provisions, or be placed in some fresh institutional structure that would provide fuller satisfaction for the interests of all parties. The case in principle for its role in establishing a more adequate international legal order for energy trade, including the issue of transit, and investment in the Pan-European Space, and for supplying dispute resolution mechanisms, has been abundantly underlined by the recent events. New issues include the future of gas pricing, and in particular whether the gas price should be de-linked from the oil price, given the emergence and likely growing importance of a spot market price for LNG supplies.

Statement of the Secretary General of the Energy Charter Secretariat on the Recent Developments in the Russia-Ukraine Gas Dispute

Since 7 January 2009, no Russian gas is flowing at the entry and exit points of the Ukrainian system. For the first time in history, the Ukrainian gas transportation system, which is the largest gas transit system worldwide, is not providing any transit.

It is worth reiterating that the principle of uninterrupted transit is one of the core principles of the Energy Charter. While Article 7(5) of the Energy Charter Treaty specifically requires member countries to "*...secure established flows of Energy Materials and Products to, from or between the Areas of other contracting Parties*"; Article 16 of the draft Transit Protocol requires each member state to take necessary measures "*...to expeditiously restore the normal operation of such Transit*" in case of interruption, reduction or stoppage of transit flows.

The Secretary General urges all parties involved to focus their efforts on restoring full operation of gas transit via Ukraine and a speedy resumption of the established gas transit flows. In doing so, all parties involved should further ensure the necessary communication and cooperation between the system operators involved to restore the system. Furthermore, the parties involved should prevent the disputes of national or international contractual and legal claims to be a hindrance for dealing with issues of vital importance and settle these disputes at the appropriate time.

Regarding the disputed transit issues, the Secretariat invites the parties involved to consider the conciliation procedure according to Article 7(7) of the Energy Charter Treaty, which provides a forum to look for solutions of these issues between the parties to the dispute. The Secretary General has found the former President of the International Gas Union, George Verberg, also former CEO of the Dutch gas company Gasunie, available to lead such conciliation efforts.

Source: Remarks by André Mernier, Secretary General of the Energy Charter Secretariat, 9 January 2009 (http://www.encharter.org).

Among the key questions to be explored include how might the recent extreme gas price volatility, following the oil price with around half a year of time-lag, be reduced? Might there be introduced into long-term contracts a corridor of minimum and maximum prices for long-term supply contracts within which prices could fluctuate? Could the protracted negotiations over the transit protocol be concluded, with possibly some movement from the EU side on its position that these provisions would not apply within the EU (i.e. revisit the Regional Economic Integration Organisation clause)? Should the existing dispute settlement mechanisms be adapted in some way to make their use more likely, with the addition of an early warning mechanism that could be activated by the Energy Charter secretariat? Some of these ideas seem to be in circulation at least informally in energy policy circles. Perhaps there are grounds for a fresh round of negotiations in search of a balanced outcome that would make for a more effective regime for pan-European energy markets.

The Black Sea Economic Cooperation organisation (BSEC) should in principle be able to work in favour of EaP-Rus-EU projects and policies of cooperation, with encouragement now from the EU which becomes an observer in the context of the Black Sea Synergy initiative. BSEC has an elaborate institutional structure, but its performance has been hindered by a lack of professional capacity in the permanent secretariat and the difficulty in achieving political consensus over significant decisions (with Russia often blocking proposals entailing operational constraints and commitments). For this reason the EU was careful not to grant BSEC any claims for exclusivity in developing its Black Sea Synergy programme.

The UN Economic Commission for Europe (UNECE) is the grandfather of all pan-European institutions, set up in 1947. It has steadily withered away in political significance, although it has continued to do some useful things of a highly technical character such as on customs and the transport/transit of goods. It is not plausible to look to UNECE for any new initiative of importance, given the development of the enlarged EU itself, its bilateral relationships and the other (mostly more recent) pan-European organisations as discussed above.

Conclusion: Several pan-European multilateral organisations should in principle be supporting cooperation between all parties. Of the existing organisations only the EBRD has established an important niche activity that all parties, including Russia, seem content to work with. On the other hand Russia seeks to marginalise or ignore other organisations that should be serving key functions (especially the Energy Charter Treaty and OSCE), while the BSEC and UNECE find it difficult to establish or build significant roles. However both the OSCE and BSEC could see their role in economic affairs enhanced by various of the proposals discussed in this paper. The recent gas crisis further poses the question whether some revision or enhancement of the Energy Charter Treaty could provide fuller satisfaction for the interests of all parties and thus help establish a more effective order in the pan-European energy domain and provide fuller satisfaction for the interests of all parties.

14. THE GLOBAL FINANCIAL AND ECONOMIC CRISIS

The exposure of Central and East European economies to the global crisis has dramatically increased in the last few weeks and months, as the gravity of the global crisis has deepened and the vulnerabilities of this wider European region have become more apparent. Exchange rate depreciations on the order of 35 to 50% have been seen already in Russia, Poland and Ukraine, three major economies with fundamentally different starting points. So far these depreciations could be seen more or less as warranted adjustments. However the risk of true financial crisis, and domino effect contagion between all countries of the region, is now evident, due to large exposure in these countries to hard currency debt while their own currencies have plunged. European banks such as Raiffeisen and other major actors, having initially been criticised for aggravating the situation by withdrawing funds from these countries, are now exposed to the huge debt default risks. The calls for a concerted European response are now being made, as evidenced by the mini-summit of the EU's new member states of the region on 1 March, preceding the plenary EU summit the same day.

The striking feature of the present situation for the purpose of this report is that Russia, in spite of its own difficulties, has rushed in with financial assistance to Belarus, Ukraine and Kyrgyzstan, following the IMF in Belarus and Ukraine. The EU led a major donor effort in favour of Georgia after the August war, but has not so far acted otherwise in response to the region's financial crises, beyond supporting actions of the EBRD to recapitalise banks and of the IMF in supplying macro-financial aid.

The question that is now posed is whether the EU and Russia should coordinate their actions in the region, in association with the IMF. As in the case of almost every other field of possible action reviewed in this report, the starting situation is characterised by stand-off or competition in the attitudes of Russia, whose leadership is making speeches about being 'alone' in their willingness to come to the help of its neighbours, in spite of its own difficulties. The EU has since the 1990s become accustomed to co-funding macro-financial assistance to countries in its neighbourhood with the IMF and to some extent also the World Bank. The EU has let the IMF and World Bank often take the lead in defining the conditionalities. It would not be difficult technically for Russia to join the process in a similar manner.

Could the gravity of the present crisis become instrumental in engineering a change in Russian willingness to enter into truly cooperative actions? Russia will want to have its loans reimbursed. It will also want to avoid a spectacle of economic collapse around its borders, with the manifest risk of domino effects between countries, not excluding Russia. At a very recent public conference in Brussels, both Commission officials and a Russian ambassador were heard agreeing that there absolutely had to be coordination. Could this even become the tipping point for a re-assessment of Russian willingness to enter into deeper regional cooperation with the EU, Eastern Europe and Central Asia? The preceding sections of this report have drawn up a long list of important conceivable cooperative actions, offering in principle important synergetic benefits; yet in almost every case there is resistance on the part of Russia based on a competitive logic seeking to reconstruct a sphere of influence; and resistance by countries such as Ukraine which deeply distrust Russia.

Conclusion: The deepening financial and economic crisis in Eastern Europe and Central Asia now sees Russia rushing in with financial aid to several countries of the region, alongside interventions by the IMF, and with the new member states of the EU calling for a more active response by the EU in favour of both themselves and neighbouring non-member states. The case for coordinated responses, including conditionalities, is manifest to avoid inconsistent actions and secure synergetic benefits. Such coordination between Russia on the one hand, and the IMF, EU and the countries concerned on the other, is not yet happening. But perhaps initiatives along these lines could, with some bold political leadership, be engineered; even more tantalising is the idea that this could become the tipping point to set in motion a change of strategic attitudes and thence a cascade of other cooperative actions of the kinds outlined in earlier sections of this report.